A Remarkable Political Movement

A Remarkable Political Movement

V. Shanmuganathan

DIVE IN THE OCEAN OF KNOWLEDGE
Ocean Books

Ocean Books Pvt. Ltd.
ISO 9001:2015 Publishers

Published by
Ocean Books (P) Ltd.
4/19 Asaf Ali Road,
New Delhi-110 002 (INDIA)
e-mail: prabhatbooks@gmail.com

ISBN 978-81-8430-257-8
A REMARKABLE POLITICAL MOVEMENT
by V. Shanmuganathan

Edition
2025

Price
₹ 300.00 (Rupees Three Hundred only)

Printed at
Yash Printographics, Noida

L.K. ADVANI
CHAIRMAN
BJP Parliamentary Party

सत्यमेव जयते

Dated : Nov. 01, 2013

Message

The Bharatiya Janata Party formally took shape in 1980. But those active in the party today are acutely conscious of the fact that their political *yatra* actually began shortly after the country was liberated from British rule, and immediately after the Constituent Assembly formally adopted the Constitution.

The Constitution was finalized in 1950. It was in 1951 that Dr. Syama Prasad Mookerjee launched the Bharatiya Jana Sangh. The BJP is continuing the work of the Jana Sangh. For all these six and a half decades since independence we all have been exerting with a missionary zeal to make Bharat the greatest country in the world. Political parties are generally power-oriented. But BJP is a mission-oriented party.

I have known Shri V. Shanmuganathan since 1970 as a dedicated, committed activist, originally of the R.S.S., and now also of the BJP. I am happy he has penned down his experiences in politics. I have no doubt readers would find the book educative and inspiring.

L. K. Advani

(L.K. ADVANI)

RES. : 30, PRITHVIRAJ ROAD, NEW DELHI-110001
TEL. : 23794124, 23794125 • FAX : 23013142

Rajnath Singh
Member of Parliament
(Lok Sabha)

सत्यमेव जयते

Dated : August 14, 2013

Message

I am happy to know that Thiru V. Shanmugnathan has come up with a book named 'A Remarkable Political Movement' which is essentially a collection of essays highlighting the rise of the BJP as a political force in the country. He also gives a ring side view of Parliament and explores the roots of BJP's political journey.

The BJP is not merely a political party but a political movement inspired by the principles of 'Bharat' (India) and 'Bharatiyata' (Indianness). 'Bharatiyata' or our Indian value system is not merely a matter of cultural pride but it also serves as the source of its inherent and latent strength.

As we in the Bharatiya Janata Party are committed to 'Cultural Nationalism' it is quite natural for us to have a great sense of pride for our rich heritage and vibrant culture. We believe in 'Hindutva' which has nothing to do with any particular religion. 'Hindutva' is the cultural symbol of anything and everything which is associated with Indian culture and its long cherished traditions.

'Hindutva' is also the source of economic prosperity, our ability to fight, and intellectual prowess. It spreads the message of social equality and, above all, Hindutva is the symbol of India's way of life. The Supreme Court of India has also expatiated upon Hindutva on these lines. Hindutva is therefore an inspirational and liberal thought.

Our economic thought is guided by the philosophy of 'Integral Humanism' which was expounded by our great visionary ideologue Pt. Deendayal Upadhyay. The idea of integral humanism does not believe in uncontrolled consumption and unchecked exploitation but it believes in striking a balance and harmony. The uplift of the poor, deprived and oppressed class, the dalits and other backward sections of the society is the focal point of our economic thought. Under the philosophy of 'Integral Humanism', the concept of 'Antyodaya', that is, the emancipation of the person standing on the lowest rung of the societal ladder, takes us to the fullness to our ideology.

Today India is facing multiple crises and the crisis of credibility has made the situation even worse. The credibility of politics needs to be restored. The BJP has also committed itself to good governance and development. Our cherished aim has been to raise the standards of living of the common people by taking development to newer heights. During the NDA regime we accomplished many outstanding achievements under the astute leadership of Shri Atal Bihari Vajpayee as the prime minister of India. There are many states where we are in power today and I am happy to note that the BJP led state governments have been performing exceedingly well.

I would like to congratulate Thiru V Shanmugnathan who has covered some of these aforementioned issues in his book. I hope that this book will be of immense help to the people who want to decode the BJP as a political thought and also as a nationalist movement.

(RAJNATH SINGH)

Off : 11, Ashok Road, New Delhi-110001 • Ph : +91-11-23005700
• Fax : +91-11-23005787
Res : 38, Ashok Road, New Delhi-110001 • Ph : +91-11-23353881, 23354184
• E-mail : 38ashokroad@gmail.com

Narendra Modi
Chief Minister, Gujarat State

सत्यमेव जयते

Date: 14-06-2013

Message

Leading the Government with the welfare of all including the under privileged and down trodden people, at the heart can be termed as the real politics. It is not merely being in power with propagandas for attracting people. The quality of being selfless and being concerned for all rather than being that for me and mine, is essential for making the "politics" more meaningful and amicable. Having faith in this ideology can only lead to the formation of the party with the purpose and difference which is very essential for nation building.

The greatness and selflessness of the ancestors like Dr. Hedgewarji, Syama Prasad Mookerjee, Pandit Deendayal Upadhyayji, Atalji have blessed and nurtured BJP in terms of ideology and implementation. This is at the root of all the virtues visible in BJP *karyakartas* like commitment and dedication for the nation above the self interests, ambitions and necessities. With this pure emotion at the heart, BJP has succeeded in carving a new path of selfless polity in this political arena of deteriorating values.

It is indeed a matter of great inspiration to have these contents in the book "A Remarkable Political Movement" written by V. Shanmuganathan, a true *Swayamsevak* of RSS.

I convey my warm greetings to V. Shanmuganathan for his thoughtful creation in form of a book "A Remarkable Political Movement" having the potential to lead, inspire and activate the nation in the direction of growth and development with intact identity. I extend my best wishes for all its success.

(Narendra Modi)

To,
Shri V. Shanmuganathan,
BJP Headquarters,
11, Ashoka Road,
New Delhi-110001

नेता प्रतिपक्ष
(लोकसभा)

Leader of Opposition
(Lok Sabha)

सत्यमेव जयते

सुषमा स्वराज
Sushma Swaraj

23 July 2013

Message

I am very happy to know that a compilation of articles on the works done by the Bharatiya Janata Party written by Shri V Shanmuganathan are being published in the form of a book, 'A Remarkable Political Movement'.

As the Bharatiya Janata Party (BJP) sets on the 34th year of its eventful history, it can look back with pride. It is no small achievement to emerge as one of the leading Parties in India's political spectrum in such a short time. From only two seats in the Lok Sabha in 1984, the BJP now stands tall, occupying the political centre stage with the other much older political parties. This has been possible only because of the tireless efforts of its leaders and workers and tremendous support the party received from the masses on its Principles and Policies. Apart from making India a strong and self reliant Nation, the BJP is strongly committed to the protection of our social values and cultural heritage.

Through the various articles published in the book, the author has attempted to portray all the good work done by the BJP inside Parliament and in the States it has ruled. Besides, the book also contains some very absorbing articles on India's rich cultural, spiritual and literary life, without that, it would be difficult to understand India or its people.

I convey my best wishes to the Author on this occasion.

(Sushma Swaraj)

Off : 44, Parliament House, New Delhi-110001 • Tel. : +91-11-2301-6705 • Fax : 2301-7470

Res : 8, Safdarjung Lane, New Delhi-110011 • Tel. : +91-11-2379-4344, 2379-4044

ARUN JAITLEY
Member of Parliament
Leader of Opposition
(Rajya Sabha)

सत्यमेव जयते

43, Parliament House,
New Delhi-110001
Tel. : 23016707, 23034883
Fax : 23793433

September 16, 2013

Message

I have had the privilege of reading the manuscript of your book "A Remarkable Political Movement". Your book is a journey which deals with creation of a political movement namely the Bharatiya Jana Sangh and its subsequent *avatar* the Bharatiya Janata Party.

You have used your political experience as a *Karyakarta* to compile the various aspects of the biography of a political party. The ideology of a political party represented by its stand on various issues signifies the personality of the Party. Its top leaders become the face of the political party; its internal democratic functioning and its concern for the country give to it the nationalistic credentials. Your book is an account of all these factors written by someone who has an inside view of the developments. I compliment you for your research in authoring the book. I am sure this book will be a valuable addition to all the libraries.

Yours sincerely,

(Arun Jaitley)

Shri V. Shanmuganathan,
New Delhi

Residence : A-44, Kailash Colony, New Delhi-110048 • Tel. : 29237483, 29244587, 29248212 • Fax : 29232358 • Website : http://rajyasabha.nic.in • http://rajyasabhahindi.nic.in

Ramlal
National General Secretary
(Org.)

भारतीय जनता पार्टी
Bharatiya Janata Party

Dated : Nov. 01, 2013

Message

Shri V Shanmuganathan has written this book mainly to highlight the positive contributions of BJP to our country and people.

Dr. Syama Prasad Mookerjee's sacrifice for the unity and integrity of our country from Kashmir to Kanyakumari is a marvelous example.

Our party fought against the rule of emergency to protect the democratic values of the country. Bharatiya Janata Party participated in the struggle for Ramjanma Bhoomi and Ramsetu for safeguarding the cultural values of our motherland.

Atalji as Prime Minister took great initiative for the successful nuclear experiment in Pokhran for arousing the spirit of national self respect.

Integral humanism is the heart beat of BJP. Its concept and practice is the lifeline of its very existence. It is the guiding force behind a long list of successful campaigns by the party ever since its inception. Right from the mass campaign against the cow slaughters, the Liberation struggle of Goa, to have made the world sit up and take note of its strongest ever protests against the Chinese aggression in 1962, all this and more stand a testimony to the BJP's grit of determination and its commitment to its principles.

Distinctly at variance against other political parties, BJP chose to launch its own unique way of political mass campaigns. *Yatras* are age old concept of national intergration in our country. By modernizing the concept of *yatras* Shri L.K. Advani strode over the length and breadth of our motherland to strengthen social harmony and unity. The National Democratic Alliance government under the leadership of Shri Atal Bihari Vajpayee is appreciated for good governance. The author of this book has written about the special care and concern shown by BJP ruled states government's for *Gaon, Gareeb* and *Kisan*.

This book deals with wide range of issues. It covers BJP's contribution inside and outside Parliament. 'A Remarkable Political Movement' is a gift to everyone who wants to know about the concrete achievements of BJP.

Yours,

(Ramlal)

Introduction

This book comes at a time when India is again looking at the Bharatiya Janata Party (BJP) as blooming lotus of hope. For almost ten years, it has been out of power in the Centre, the Party has run model governments in Gujarat, Madhya Pradesh and Chhattisgarh etc. These turnaround stories can be beacons for the rest of India. As the misgovernment of the UPA-II drives India into a morass, the people are nostalgically looking back upon the Vajpayee years. They also find the present BJP best placed to replace the UPA in the Centre.

The now-soured 'India Story', which grew under the NDA-rule, was no accidental episode. It could be attributed to the conviction, commitment and control structure of the Party. The BJP demonstrated its capability of harmonizing distinct elements in the NDA coalition. The 'India Story' happened during the NDA years, because Vajpayee government believed in unlocking the potential in every facet of India through enabling environment. It espoused a vision of resurgent India. By contrast the UPA believes in making India a handout state.

The difference that the BJP in power made is attributable to the philosophy it nurtured while nowhere in the sight of power. Dr. Syama Prasad Mookerjee, the founder of *Jana Sangh*, resigned from Nehru cabinet as non-Congress member. He led to the Opposition, tiny in size comparable to Congress, but greater in conviction. His famous debates in the Lok Sabha, which put Nehru on the defence, remain a legend. The sapling planted by him has grown into the large tree. Its branches overarch from Gujarat to Andaman & Nicobar Islands and from Punjab to Karnataka. It is a testimony to its vitality and mass appeal. These are expected to increase as the BJP goes for a generational shift and regains control of its party structure.

This concise book portrays the vignettes of what I call a 'Remarkable Political Movement'. It draws upon my experiences in social and political activism. The nationalist ideology I was drawn towards in my impressionable years was uncommon in Tamil Nadu. But this remarkable movement, anchored to Indian view of nationalism, captivated my imagination. Subsequently, it became the preoccupation of my life. While still young, I came across an extraordinary letter written by Pandit Deendayal Upadhyay to his maternal uncle. The letter succinctly explains why the ideologue of Jana Sangh wanted to dedicate his life for cause of the nation. Pt. Upadhyay says, "any individual may achieve a very high degree of progress, but that has no significance unless his motherland too, registers corresponding progress. That is why so many Karyakartas have renounced their personal ambition and dedicated themselves wholly and solely to the uplift of the people. This will hardly be any kind of sacrifice; it will rather be an investment. It is like providing the far of society with manure. We are nowadays interested only in reaping the harvest and have forgotten to provide the field with manure. There is thus the danger of our land becoming barren and unproductive. Can we not forego a few worthless ambitions for the protection and benefit of our own people?"

The letter turned a refreshing chapter in my life. It was an exposition that giving makes one nobler than taking. The spirit of dedication & sacrifice present in the national life of pre-independent India had dissipated after independence. The urge to lay down everything for freedom of India had been substituted with quest for power. There were newer complexities to deal with in social, political and economic fields. The discourse became divisive rather than integrative. That was the irony that unfolded to my generation born within a few years of independence.

But fortunately not all was lost. The spirit of idealist nationalism reasserted itself. Independent India produced its first martyr in the form of Dr. Syama Prasad Mookerjee (1953). Dr. Mookerjee passed away in Kashmir on June 23, 1953 in extra-judicial detention of Sheikh Abdullah government. He had gone to the crown state of India to affirm the unity of India. This unity had been denied not merely by the Abdullah government in Srinagar but ironically Nehru government in New Delhi. Dr. Mookerjee – in his series of correspondences with Nehru and Sheikh Abdullah- found Nehru blaming the people of Jammu as troublemakers. The people of Jammu, in reality, were agitating for complete unification with India. It is a poetic justice that while Dr. Mookerjee shines in his martyrdom, Nehru's reputation ended in ruination as a result of Chinese aggression, 1962.

I was a child when Dr. Mookerjee passed away. I have heard & read about the moving tale of his martyrdom. Though I did not have the opportunity to see Pt. Deendayal Upadhyay either but I read his landmark work 'Integral Humanism'. The appeal of his philosophy attracted me to the fold of the Jana Sangh. I, however, had the privilege of coming in close contact of Atal Bihari Vajpayee.

The charismatic personality of Atalji–his soberness, magnanimity, love of the people drew me nearer to him. His ability to take people of different backgrounds on board is remarkable. As the Prime Minister of India (1998-2004) he managed a coalition of 24-parties in National Democratic Alliance (NDA). He thus proved his detractors wrong that the BJP was an exclusivist party. Atal-*ji* is a poet who is deeply rooted in the Indian ethos. Before the BJP came to power it was criticized as bereft of any economic agenda. But while the BJP came to power, it proved its critics wrong absolutely. In the NDA government, the BJP always retained the Finance Portfolio. The economic policies of the BJP put India into high growth, low inflation and low interest rate trajectory. The NDA government took the fallouts of East Asia Crisis (1997) and post-Pokhran II sanctions in a stride through Resurgent India Bonds and India Millennium Deposits.

Infrastructure like Highways and Rural Roads got a priority under the NDA government. Both were results of Atal-*ji's* vision.

While Congress specializes in naming every road, bridges, hospitals, schemes and sports tournaments after members of Gandhi-Nehru dynasty, Atal *ji* in all modesty refuse to perpetuate his name thus. The rural road connectivity project was named *Pradhan Mantri Gram Sadak Yojana (PMGSY)* and *Golden Quadrilateral Project*.

Now nearly ten years out of power, the BJP has still played its role as a strong and responsible Opposition inside and outside Parliament. The UPA government's reign is marred by rampant corruption, wasteful expenditure on harebrained schemes, misusing the government agencies, tendency to encroach upon the rights of the states and sagging confidence on the economy etc. The BJP, as the principal Opposition party, has consistently kept the heat on the government. The Party in Opposition has fought a crusade against corruption, weak internal security, tepid response to Pakistan-sponsored terror and stood in defence of federalism, freedom of speech & expression and good governance.

This book was originally written as a series of articles over the last few years. It is divided into four sections. The first section *BJP- A Distinctive and Significant Force* delves upon the BJP's attainments in field of governance and some political notes. Second section *Ring Side View of Parliament* deals with important issues raised by the BJP in Parliament. The third & last section, *Social and Cultural Background, The Roots* are the collection of my jottings on spirituality, arts and culture as resources of national life.

I would consider my sincere efforts rewarded, if the readers find the book ennobling.

—V. Shanmuganathan

11, Ashoka Road
New Delhi-110001
e-mail ID : vsnathan7666@gmail.com
Mob. : 09811432960

Content

Social & Cultural Background

The Roots

Dr. S.P. Mookerjee and Pt. Deendayal Upadhyay

BJP—A Distinct and Significant Force

Atal Bihari Vajpayee: The Finest Prime Minister of India

Atalji has a pleasing, irresistible, magnetic and appealing personality. He commands respect. He attracts people because of his sweet behaviour. Atalji is able to understand the finer feelings, delicacies and sensitivities of different sections of the society. In his long career as a writer, editor, political thinker, Member of Parliament, Cabinet Minister and The Prime Minister, he evolved as a universal personality. One of the leading newspapers in Delhi wrote about him after the 2004 elections, "history will remember Atal Bihari Vajpayee as one of India's finest prime ministers."

The National democratic alliance government under the leadership of Shri Atal Bihari Vajpayee can be described as a government that changed India's economic and political scenario. The greatness of Atalji's leadership was always nation centric and focused on the welfare of the people. Atal Bihari Vajpayee is appreciated by one and all because of his unique style of functioning. He had set a role model for good governance. It was always participatory, consensus oriented, transparent, responsive, effective and efficient. It was also equitable and inclusive and followed the rule of law. It assured that corruption is eliminated, the views of minorities are taken into account and that the voices of the most vulnerable in society are heard in decision making. It is also responsive to the present and future needs of society.

Even today, I remember the words of late CN Annadurai. He was the first non-Congress CM of Tamil Nadu who fought against the imposition of Hindi as the official language. He spoke in the Parliament after hearing the speech of Atalji, "if this is the attitude, we are not against Hindi language". Because of his broad vision aversions were removed. People with various backgrounds were won over by his majestic handling of issues and emotions. Even today Vaiko, leader of MDMK, often quotes the name of Atalji as a leader with kindness and compassion. Even today many people say that they were inspired by the leadership qualities of Atal Bihari Vajpayee. Because of his friendly nature, Atalji is able to connect people with various backgrounds. Every nook and corner of our country knows him as a mass leader with great magnanimity. It was the first time since Independence that a non Congress government had completed its term under his leadership.

Chinna Pazham, an uneducated lady who belongs to a socially weaker section of our society did a lot of service in Madurai. She has worked for the upliftment of poor people, particularly dalit women. Atalji came to Tamil Nadu as Prime Minister and gave an award to her for her selfless service. Not only that, after the award was given, on the dais, he touched the feet of that lady. He appreciated her wonderful attitude of care, concern and compassion about the sufferings of others and helping them. Next day, all papers of Tamil Nadu published the photo of Atalji touching the feet of a village woman in front of TV cameras on the dais in the public function held at Madurai. No doubt, every Tamilian's heart was moved and overwhelmed by the supreme affection of Atalji. People of the entire State, cutting across the party divisions, en masse were immensely pleased by the behaviour of Atalji.

Atalji is considered as a soft person. But he stunned the world when a series of nuclear tests at Pokhran were conducted in May 1998 under his leadership. His bus journey to Pakistan in February 1999 was widely acclaimed and admired as a sincere initiative towards solving the outstanding problems of the subcontinent. India's honesty has made an impact on the pragmatic world community. Later, when this gesture of friendship was replied back by a betrayal of faith in Kargil, Atalji successfully handled the situation by repulsing the intruders from the Indian soil.

Atalji has a remarkable persuasive skill. When Tamil Nadu and Karnataka were fighting for Cauveri water, he called the Chief Ministers of both the states, heard their problems patiently and solved it amicably during his period. Then he sincerely tried for linking the various rivers to solve the problem of flood and drought.

During Vajpayee's government India experienced one of its fastest periods of economic growth. India became an emerging power in information technology due to the reform programmes executed under his guidance. Vajpayeeji's philosophy is that every region, every community and every citizen in our country should enjoy the fruits of India's prosperity and progress. In this background the six years of BJP led NDA rule created 6.2 crore jobs. "Golden Quadrilateral" connecting the four metro cities of India was completed within a period of 5 years. The road construction reached 11 km of highway per day. The "Delhi Metro" project was launched by Vajpayee in 2002.

For the first time, 3.5 crore farmers got "Kissan Credit Card" along with insurance cover for each card holder. NDA introduced low cost airlines in 2004. When NDA left, India's foreign exchange stood at 118 billion dollars.

India's Former Prime Minister, Shri Atal Bihari Vajpayee is respected worldwide as India's most influential and charismatic politician'. The world recognises him as an outstanding leader who achieved economic development and a historic peace process with Pakistan. After 2004 election results, he revealed his heart and made a touching reference. He had said, "Victory and defeat are part of life which are to be viewed with equanimity. My party and alliance have lost, but

India has won. Dear countrymen, we have given up office but not our responsibility to serve the nation . We have lost an election, but not our determination." This undaunted resolve and unshakeable commitment with hard work will bring a better future for the Party as well as our nation.

> Atal Bihari Vajpayee is respected worldwide as India's most influential and charismatic politician. The world recognises him as an outstanding leader who achieved economic development and a historic peace process with Pakistan. After 2004 election results, he revealed his heart and made a touching reference. He had said "Victory and defeat are part of life which are to be viewed with equanimity. My party and alliance have lost, but India has won."

❑

Highest Good is the Target of BJP

For some time, a section of media has launched propaganda campaign purporting as if everything was wrong with BJP. A scenario is created where ranking leaders are projected to be fighting among themselves. There is a war of letters and accusations. This is a deliberate attempt by some sections of the media launched by political rivals to destroy the patriotic image of BJP. What is the real position? Where is the heartbeat of BJP? How does it reverberate? It is the faith and ideological commitment of thousands of leaders, lakhs of karyakartas and crores of admirers, supporters and sympathisers that forms the bedrock of BJP.

A few days back, one of our leaders travelled from Delhi to Shajahanpur in Uttar Pradesh by train. Since the train was expected to reach at 3.30 A. M, he wanted that somebody should receive him on the station. So, he telephoned them before starting and then reminded them in the morning. Early morning he got a special SMS saying, "Sir, don't worry. You are coming for the first time and so are concerned about your reaching the place. We are about100 people waiting for you on the platform since last night". The leader was emotionally moved as he saw them waiting at the station for the whole night just to receive him.Complementing them the leader asked, "You people are wonderful, what made you wait for me for such a long time?" One of them spontaneously spoke, "Sir,

BJP for us is nationalism, uncompromising natonalism. We are ready to make even supreme sacrifice for the nation. Night stay at Railway station was mainly to receive your good self with affection". Every one was happy with the remark and warmth shown to the special guest of honour.

There have been great pillars of inspiration in the Party like Dr. Syama Prasad Mookerjee and Pt. Deendayal Upadhyay. People were encouraged for doing dedicated work citing their examples. Even today, there are replicas of these great leaders at every place in large numbers.

Recently, some prominent people of Chhattisgarh State came to Delhi. They talked of a rare example of political work. Mr. Nandakumar Sai was the state president of BJP. He went to a village predominently inhabited by tribals. It was the evening time when he saw them drinking alcohol. Most of them were fully drunk. He told them, "Please don't drink. It is injurious to health. It could be fatal." But they made fun of him. One of them even shouted at him. "Can you stop taking salt along with food that you eat. Just like salt, the drinks are essential for us." Nand Kumar Sai asked them, "O. K. If I stop eating salt would you people stop drinking liquor?" The people around him told that, "First, you stop it for one year then we will follow you." Nand Kuamr Sai stopped eating salt from that very moment. Eighteen years have passed he has not tasted salt. The village people by seeing the example of this man forsake the habit of drinking liquor. There are numerous such examples that need to be highlighted as part of a positive discourse. Unfortunately, negative propaganda is unleashed about BJP. No TV channel would show the determination of Nand Kumar Sai.

Shri Kabindra Purkayastha is Member of Parliament from Silchar in Assam. He was a middle school teacher and father of two children. In due course, the middle school became higher secondary school, and then he became the Principal. He joined BJP. As a teacher he was impressed by the concept of BJP. He immersed himself in the ideaology of the Party. He mused, "Here was a great civilization, glory of which spread from Sri Lanka to Java and Japan and from Tibet and Mangolia to China and Siberia. It weathered the storms of Huns, Shakas and Turks. Through a 1000-Year resistance this country bled immensely but never bowed. Its civilization survived through the heroic efforts of its valient men and women like the builders of the Vijaynagar Empire, Shivaji, Rana Pratap and Guru Govind Singh and countless other heroes and martyrs. In more recent times, the good work has been carried on by Lokmanya Tilak, Mahatma Gandhi, Dr. Keshav Baliram Hedgewar, Dr. Syama Prasad Mookerjee, Pt. Deendayal Upadhyay and many others. So we must contribute our time and energy to make a brave new India with a promise to establish "Ram Rajya".

Imbued by such great thoughts, Shri Kabindra Purkayastha resigned from the school and joined Jan Sangh as a full time worker. He organised Bharatiya Jan Sangh and later the BJP in various parts of the state contesting elections. In the year 1997, he became the Minister of Communication in the Central Government. He traced a letter written by Shri Atal Bihari Vajpayee, as a Member of Parliament in 1987 to the then Minister of Communication Shri Arjun Singh. Atalji had requested him to release a stamp on Dr. Hedgewar during the latter's birth centenary as a mark of respect. Arjun Singh had rejected the proposal. Shri Kabindra felt that an injustice had been done to a great visionary like Dr. Hedgewar. He took the matter to the Prime Minister Atal Bihari Vajpayee and told him that the stamp should be released by him. Atalji gave him the necessary go ahead. With his special efforts, 33 lakh stamps were sold on the day of release. It had beaten all the previous records. Shri Kabindra is so happy even today about this achievement.

The quality of the BJP cadre is exemplary. They join BJP to serve the motherland and not to loot it. They are known for selflessness, which is unique in the politics of today. The nation can rely on them for anything and everything. No malicious propaganda can curtail the saga of faith and commitment.

> There have been great pillars of inspiration in the Party like Dr. Syama Prasad Mookerjee and Pt. Deendayal Upadhyay. People were encouraged for doing dedicated work citing their examples. Even today, there are replicas of these great leaders at every place in large numbers.

❑

BJP—Gears Up for Greater Performance

Spectacular achievement is always preceded by spectacular preparations. Various state assembly elections and general elections are fast nearing. Madhya Pradesh, Chhattisgarh, Rajasthan and Delhi Assembly Elections are going to take place in the month of November 2013. We are in favour of conducting elections for Jharkhand Assembly during the same period, clubbed with other states instead of extending the President's rule. Sixteenth Lok Sabha elections can take place any time due to the prevailing political uncertainty.

Congress led UPA-II is *sinking and stinking* everyday by getting involved in corrupt practices, scams and open public loot. "Aam Admi" is terribly annoyed over the misrule of Congress Party. The stress and sufferings of common people are increasing day by day, mainly due to rocket high prices of essential commodities and food price inflation.

On the Ground Level

BJP focuses its attention to highlight the painful miseries of underprivileged and poverty-stricken people. Karyakarthas of BJP echo the public anger by series of agitational programmes on the ground and in the streets.

Thousands of advocates, doctors, labourers, farmers,

fishermen, weavers, textile workers have been organised in different parts of the country. *Jail Bharo, Bharat Bandh* drew the attention of the masses at the grass-root level. The same public agony and hardship was expressed by our elected representatives in the various State Assemblies of the country. In total, there are 924 Legislative Assembly and Council Members. There are 164 Members of Parliament, both Lok Sabha and Rajya Sabha together. There are 53 Mayors in various city corporations and 95 district panchayat presidents.

Inside Parliament

They have played a valuable role on several issues like the bill against women harassment, land acquisition, communal violence, FDI in retail sector, miserable migration of Hindus from Pakistan and Bangladesh, tragedy of Tamils in Sri Lanka, failure of economic policies, inflation, Telengana, brutal killing of Indian Army soldiers by Pakistan, violence in Assam and other places. BJP raised it's voice for the causes of farmers, poor, youth, Scheduled Castes and Scheduled Tribes. It is continuously fighting for Ganga-Yamuna purification and linking of major rivers for the benefit of village people, mainly the farmers.

The Strength of BJP

BJP is taking special initiatives to reach all sections of the people, by taking the message of value-based politics. It is enlarging it's base to bring all sections of our people, with the concept of *Sarva Vyapi* and *Sarva Sparshi*. It is evident in the latest membership campaign programme. Membership of BJP at the national level as on 15 March, 2013 has crossed 3 crores 12 lakhs 24 thousands and one hundred seven. BJP has good organizational functioning in all the 35 states and 633 districts. Out of 8,30,866 polling booths in the whole country, BJP has got booth level functioning committees in 6,82.069 polling booths. At present, BJP is ruling in five states and with coalition partners two states are governed by the BJP.

There are only 370 days left for the coming 16th Lok Sabha elections and even lesser time left for different state assembly elections. BJP is preparing itself to go to people with policies and programmes of the party. In the coming months, the Karyakartas will go from village to village and house to house. Karyakartas of BJP are going to personally contact lakhs and lakhs of people through this *Maha Abhyan,* the mass contact programme. They intend to inform the people about the wrong economic policies and the corrupt practices of the Congress rule. Time is short and works are more. In BJP we have to concentrate our day to day efforts to make the organization ready and perfect.

Karyakartas

The new team at the all-India level has taken up the work. Karyakartas with enormous leadership capabilities could be the formal leaders, driving the party to achieve success. Ideological conviction, discipline, organizational skills, reaching all sections of people specially lower strata of society, encouraging good people with talents, motivating the younger generation, clarity of vision, innovation, effective communication, democratic style of functioning, etc. are some of the qualities that need to be cultivated for successful functioning of the party. There are large number of Karyakartas committed to serve the party for their entire life.

The Way Forward

Thoughts expressed recently by prominent leaders of BJP are very important for the electoral victory of the party. In one of the recently concluded all India meet, Smt. Sushma Swaraj spoke, *"We have a good number of capable people in our party and they have legitimate political ambitions. But there are only limited number of seats and we can give ticket to only one person on a seat. So those who do not get the ticket to contest, must remember that they also should work hard with the party candidate and win the elections. Once the BJP forms the government and then there will be many posts to offer those who could not contest. The active participation of every one will make BJP to come to power and for that each member, specially the youth, should visit maximum villages and meet people and maintain regular personal contact. Unity of mind at every level and active participation of all is the need of the hour."*

BJP Chief, Shri Rajnath Singh, said that party members, including himself, should resist from speaking about their grievances to the media. BJP should rebuild it's image as the most disciplined party. Mr. L.K. Advani is repeatedly telling that there should be zero tolerance to corruption. Mr. Arun Jaitley often says that the institution of an effective lokpal and an autonomous and accountable CBI are important institutions to check corruption and the BJP stands committed for the same. *"Nation first, Party next and Self last"* is a slogan given and practiced by Mr. Nitin Gadkari. In another context, Mr. Narendra Modi said that his idea of secularism is "India First." Nothing less than India's well-being should be our goal.

Positive Support from Many Sections of People

Due to the wonderful performance of BJP-ruled State Governments, country-wide continuous work of huge number of Karyakatas and participation of people adds greater strength to BJP in the national political scene. Success always comes when thorough preparation meets opportunity. There are some positive indications from some of the regional players. In the recent times, different political party chiefs have expressed their opinions in favour of BJP. Sincere effort and contact with various like-minded political parties will bring more coalition partners and make NDA more stronger as NDA+ that is more alliance partners. India should be freed from the clenches of the cynical, sinking and stinking Congress-led UPA rule. To make it more energetic, ethusiastic and vibrant, our mother land needs to be governed by the NDA govt. Which works with the motto of Nation first.

Due to the wonderful performance of BJP-ruled State Governments, country-wide continuous work of huge number of Karyakatas and participation of people adds greater strength to BJP in the national political scene. Success always comes when thorough preparation meets opportunity.

❑

Gujarat—A Model for Development and Social Harmony

On the invitation of the Chief Minister of the State, I visted Gujarat during the last week of May 2010. On reaching Gandhinagar I met the Chief Minister, Shri Narendra Modi and discussed with him his people-centric and growth oriented efforts. He was immensely happy about the participation and cooperation of the common people in all his endeavours. I told him that the purpose of my visit mainly was to study the state of farmers, agricultural labour and the poor people vis a vis the initiatives taken by the government for rural development, eradication of poverty and improving conditions of the people of his state.

He sent a team of important persons along with me. We went around various parts of Gujarat and met ordinary farmers, village youth, politicians, scholars and various other sections of people. It was an illuminating experience. I remembered Pt. Deendayalji's writing in his political diary. He used to write that our intention may be good, we may evolve a good policy and even give an effective plan of action. It will be successful only when all the participants conceive it right in all its dimensions and execute it thoroughly, then only it can be accomplished in the real sense. Shri Narendra Modi and his team have created innovative ideas into new development models for other states to follow.

First, we went to a village called Fotiwada in Sabarkantha District to inaugurate a Krishi Mahotsava. It was a month long pre-mansoon campaign for encouraging scientific farming practices. Normally, farmers travel upto tehsil or district level agricultural officers to know about the government help in land and farm management. **Whereas in Gujarat, officers move to the villages and make themselves available to the farmers.** It is an integrated approach that includes farming practices, soil and water conservation, credit availability and marketing linkages.

As soon as we reached the village, I was invited by Dr. Amit Patel, a scientist belonging to Sardar Agricultural University to a gathering of about two hundred villagers. There was a tehsildar, district agricultural officer, horticultural officer, animal husbandry officer, cooperative bank officer, forest officer, patwari and a host of village officials. I inaugurated the Krishi Rath exhibition and spoke to the people in Hindi. The Krishi Rath is a tractor-driven mobile exhibition that moves from village to village showing the latest farming practices, value addition opportunities, innovative technologies through paintings and powerpoint presentations. The Rath halts for four hours at each village and a Kisan Sabha is organised where agricultural scientists and other experts interact with the farmers, imparting them knowledge, educating them about the various challenges, problems and solutions, resolving their queries and also receiving the feedback. There are about two hundred and twenty seven Krishi Raths to cover 18 thousand villages of Gujarat. In fact, these Kisan Mahotsavas bring together the knowledgeable agro-scientist and other expertise with the local farmers at the grass root level. It is a knowledge river that flows into the villages to enrich the farmers. Because of this wonderful initiative, not a single farmer has committed suicide in Gujarat.

A major programme of testing and analysing the health of soil is going on in all the villages of Gujarat. Through soil testing, farmers come to know about the quality of their soil and based on the data so collected they are advised the ideal crop and input mix for it. The government issues soil health cards to the farmers. These cards contain details of soil analysis with recommendations for usage of right kind of fertilizers and seeds. Lakhs of soil samples are collected and scientifically analysed and reports prepared. More than 25 lakh cards have been given to the farmers.

The state machinery is geared up to go to villages, meet the farmers, understand their problems and make available all governmental facilities. Slowly and steadily problems of the farmers are solved. It is a hard work of about one lakh government personnel at all levels from fifteen departments, banking personnels, members of cooperative societies, members of milk unions, members of input agencies like fertilizers, pesticides and seeds. It is a festival of activities varying from distribution of free fertilizer kits to the BPL farmers, animal vaccination, creation of self-help groups and the like.

The Gujarat farmers now possess a new perspective and a broader vision of their vocation owing to these mass campaigns. Gujarat's celebration of agriculture has received appreciation from the central Planning Commission and also from Dr. M S Swaminathan, the eminent agricultural scientist in the country. All in all, Gujarat has performed a miracle in agriculture. It has brought the smile of success on the faces of its farmers.

The Gujarat farmers now possess a new perspective and a broader vision of their vocation owing to these mass campaigns. Gujarat's celebration of agriculture has received appreciation from the central Planning Commission and also from Dr. M S Swaminathan, the eminent agricultural scientist in the country.

❑

How Farmers are Happy in Gujarat—A Direct Report

I met Ramesh Narayan Patel, 35, at Matwa Village, in Sabarkantha district of Gujarat. He is a graduate and father of two children. He grows fruits, specially papaya or papali. I asked him about the expenses he incurs per crop. Ramesh explained in detail; in one acre some1000 saplings are planted which he purchases from a private agency in Anand. One thousand saplings cost him Rs 8000. Then he invests Rs 8000 in manure, Rs 4000 for fertilizer, Rs 2000 for liquid fertilizer, Rs 1000 for insecticide, Rs 25000 for water by motor and drip irrigation, Rs 12000 for labour for harvesting, plucking and packing. All together Rs 60,000 is the production cost in one acre of land. Afterwards, in 18 months fruits can be plucked for 10 times. From an acre, the producer can get 300 'monds' of fruits. One 'mond' is 20 Kg, which sells for Rs 100/-His total sales touch around Rs three lakh per crop. Apart from this, he gets Rs 7500 as government subsidy. He cultivates fruits in 2.5 acre that is one hectare. Ramesh is a happy farmer growing fruits. He wishes to expand his cultivation capitalising on farmer-friendly policies of Shri Narendra Modi.

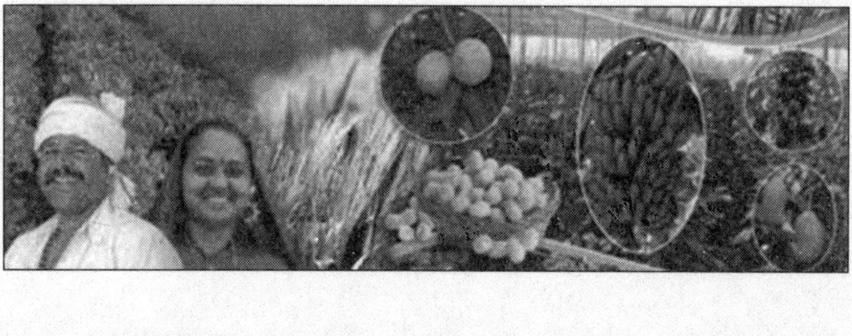

Here, I must mention about the special efforts made by Narendra Modi government for agriculture. He has ensured that the income of the farmers increases many times more by arranging adequate infrastructure for post harvest needs. Immediately after the harvest of fruits, vegetables, cereals or pulses, farmers need pre-cooling unit, cold storages, refrigerated transportation, modernised market places and outlets. Gujarat's agricultural policy offers interest subsidies and other incentives for the development of farmers.

I was glad to converse with a young educated farmer, Suresh Bhai Patel. He is a BSc (Agri) graduate and is involved in full time serious agriculture, as distinct from leisure farming. He grows capsicum that is Simla mirch. In one acre 12,000 plants can be cultivated. He spends Rs 1 60,000 for manure, fertilizer, insecticide, labour etc. Finally he is able to produce 20 tonnes of capscum worth about Rs seven lakhs. He has built a net house worth Rs. 1.6 lakh. He is an educated farmer, having a car, a tractor, cows and buffaloes and enjoys a comfortable life. Naturally, his confidence level is high.

Then, I met Dinesh, 30, a young man with a modern out look. He is educated in agricultural farming and lives in Jethpur village. He has built a green house and cultivates gerbera flowers. Government has helped him in constructing a green house for farming and he produces flowers. It gives him sufficient profit to invest further in expanding his green house cultivation of flowers. Gerberas are the most popular florist flowers available in a massive array of colours.

I had an interaction with Rathilal Patel in Rajat Kumba village. He cultivates ground nut. In one acre 800 kg of groundnuts are produced. He has to spend Rs 6000 towards production cost. He is able to earn Rs 20,000 in a period of four months. He says it is all because of the present BJP government's effective implementation of various schemes.

Hithendra Bhai produces short-term cotton in six months. One acre gives 1200 kgs to 1500 kgs of cotton yield. He can sell cotton for Rs 25 per kg. Expenses vary from Rs 15,000 to Rs. 18,000. Total sales per acre come around Rs 25,000. He says cotton production in the state has grown in recent past. Gujarat is emerging as India's largest cotton producing state and a major cotton export hub.

Mahendra produces wheat. One acre needs Rs 6,000 towards production cost. He is able to produce 14 quintals, i.e. 1400 kg per acre. He is able to sell it for Rs 20,000. The gestation period for this is four months. He is comfortable in doing wheat cultivation. I was able to feel the sweat and toil behind his success.

I met some more farmers, who produce potatoes in Dangia village of Bannattwada district. They produce 10 tons per acre by spending Rs 20,000 as cost of production. After the yield they are able to sell it for Rs 45,000. All these farmers are growing cotton, groundnut, wheat, potato, flowers and vegetables. They are all happy, confident and successful.

A village lady, Smt. Malathy Ben, from Pratap Pura village, earns Rs one lakh by selling milk. She maintains 40 cows. Each cow gives on average 15 liters of milk every day. She sells 500 liters of milk to Sagar dairy and earns a decent profit of Rs one lakh annually. She leads a dignified life with family and children.

Gujarat is the largest milk producing state. During the last five to six years agricultural growth has been faster than industrial or other services in Gujarat, improving its share in total income of the state. When I was talking to the Chief Minister, he made a lighter comment; Nano cars are cheaper than buffaloes in Gujarat. He was specially appreciating the role of 800 scientists touring the villages and motivating the farmers during the summer holidays. He called them as "Rishis of Krishi".

The Bharatiya Janata Party government has actually devoted a great deal of energy and resources in accelerating agricultural growth in the state through a broad spectrum of policy initiatives. They have improved market access, technical support, especially credit facilities, canal irrigation, judicious use of ground water, roads and other infrastructure.

Gujarat's stellar performance in agriculture needs better appreciation. Most Indian states have found it difficult to achieve even the modest plan to get four per cent agricultural growth per year. The country's growth rate for this sector is as meagre as 2.9 per cent per year. Gujarat has charted out a new course for its agrarian economy, which is exceptionally high 9.6 per cent per year besides being steady. This is mainly due to the hard work of the farmers, contribution of the agri-scientists, and above all Narendra Modi's enlightened leadership and good governance given by the Bhartiya Janata Party.

> The Bharatiya Janata Party government has actually devoted a great deal of energy and resources in accelerating agricultural growth in the state through a broad spectrum of policy initiatives. They have improved market access, technical support, especially credit facilities, canal irrigation, judicious use of ground water, roads and other infrastructure.

❑

Inclusive & Sustainable Development in Gujarat

Glimpses

- Successful interlinking of a dozen rivers.
- 24 hour uninterrupted three phase electricity to all the 18,000 villages and their households.
- Water can be seen flowing in the rivers which had dried a long back.
- Rural productivity has gone up.
- The migration to urban areas has come down.
- Per capita income of Muslims of Gujarat is the highest in the country.

- Because of administrative excellence, corruption has come down.

"What is the secret of this success in Gujarat? What is the basic factor that is responsible for the all round development of the State?" I raised these questions during my conversation with Shri Narendra Modi. Shri Modi said, "The people of Gujarat are responsible for this. Without people's participation, the impact of government run schemes would be lost. Therefore, we involve people in all developmental programmes. We have converted the adversity into opportunity." Shri Narendra Modi has indeed initiated a stable, all round development of the State with power and passion.

Gujarat was always a water scarce State. Water sector has been traditionally characterised by less rain fall, faster run off into the sea, few perennial rivers, and uneven distribution of water across regions, low ground water levels, salinity and desertification. Because of these challenges, harnessing of water was given utmost importance. Priority was given to completion of multipurpose Sardar Sarovar Narmada Project. At the same time a mega project of constructing 400 km long recharge canal to carry extra flood water to dry areas was undertaken. These efforts were supplemented by interlinking of rivers of the State and water conservation was made a people's movement. More than three lakh check dams, village and farm ponds and boribunds have been built in recent years. The age old step wells which were defunct are also being revived. The results are revealing: underground water tables are rising every year, drinking water is no longer required to be supplied through lorries or tankers. A major work to supply water to areas like Kutch district through Narmada has been completed by laying bulk line and distribution of water. Gujarat has successfully interlinked a dozen rivers including Sabarmati. Because of these efforts, water can be seen flowing in the rivers which had dried long back.

BJP government in Gujarat also paid full attention to the energy sector. Government provided new investments in power generation, transmission and distribution facilities. New transmission lines covering 58,599 km were laid. New transformers numbering 12,621across 18,000 villages were emplaced. New power plants have been launched. The biggest achievement of Narendra Modi government is 24 hour uninterrupted three phase electricity to all the 18,000 villages and their households. It has not only brightened the lives in the households but has also energised the economic activities in the villages. Its effects are enormous. The rural productivity has gone up and the migration to urban areas has come down. In the whole of India, in the energy sector, Gujarat is number one State which adds the maximum mega watts in electricity generation. Also, renewable sources of energy have been harnessed including that of wind and solar energy.

Chief Minister along with his Cabinet Ministers went to remote villages to encourage parents to enroll their children in schools. Young children in lakhs got enrolled in standard 1 all over the State. Parent Teacher Associations, self help groups and donors presented the newly enrolled children with school bags, slates, text books, note books and uniforms as gifts. To motivate the parents of the girl child, the government has introduced a scheme called "Vidya Laxmi". This scheme provides for a fixed sum when a girl gets admitted to standard 1st and 8th which can be encashed after the girl child has passed standard 5th and 12th respectively. In addition, the State also provides insurance cover to all the school and college students worth Rs one lakh. Similarly, the State is giving attention to higher education, technical, medical, engineering and other institutions of excellence to ensure better quality.

Narendra Modi launched a special scheme to improve health services by involving private doctors to undertake the task of care and safe deliveries of pregnant women. This approach has enabled the poor mothers to avail safe deliveries at the clinics of private medical practitioners who are reimbursed the cost by the government. This has led to substantial increase in safe deliveries and drastic reductions in the mortality rate of mothers and the new born. In Gujarat, if a house is registered in a woman's name the government exempts it from stamp duty. Gujarat Government attracts investments to the tune of lakhs of crores of rupees in various sectors of industry and infrastructure from domestic as well as foreign investments through a special campaigning programme called Vibrant Gujarat.

Law and order situation is far better. According to the annual report published by the National Crime Records Bureau, the crime rate is less in Gujarat as compared with other states of the country.

Gujarat handles public grievances with a humanitarian approach. In the State capital every month on 4th Thursday, applications of the aggrieved persons are invited; their grievances are registered and instantly transmitted online to the concerned authorities at the secretariat level as well as district level. Then the authorities feed their replies. In the afternoon, the CM personally listens to the applicants one by one. **The grievances as well as replies of the concerned authorities are available on his screen online.** Through video conferencing facility Shri Modi on the spot interacts with the concerned authorities at the district level in the presence of the applicant. At this time, the applicants are free to interact or interrupt the authorities. Since the Chief Minister interacts personally, the administration is on the toes. This has proved to be a very effective system of grievance reddressal.

At the district and taluka level, concerned authorities hear the public grievances on the same day and redress them. Unfortunately, malicious lies about Gujarat have been spread throughout India and the world, that Muslims are severely discriminated against and persecuted in Gujarat. It is an attempt by anti-Gujarat elements motivated by political enimity, to break the fast pace of good governance led by Shri Narendra Modi.

In 2006, the Prime Minister appointed a committee headed by Shri Rajinder Sachar. This committee made a detailed study of the economic, social and educational conditions of Muslims throughout India. This report shows that Muslims are the happiest in Gujarat. Muslims receive mainstream education. Their literacy level is fast improving. The proportion of Muslims in high government services is better when compared to Uttar Pradesh or West Bengal. Economic prosperity of an average Muslim is far better than in any other State. Per capita income of Muslims in Gujarat is also highest in the country. The Sachar Committee too accepted that Muslims of Gujarat are on firm socio-economic footing. Even the worst of critics of Modi acknowledge that corruption in the State machinery has come down.

The model of governance which Shri Narendra Modi has evolved is based upon performance and not on appeasement. When it came to fixing rational electricity charges, Shri Modi went by the professional advice given by the Electricity Regulatory Commission. Even in the midst of farmers' agitation, he did not buckle. Instead, he assured the farmers that he understood their requirements. In the following years, he implemented the surface water schemes.

In brief, one may say that development of Gujarat is all inclusive, all nourishing and all pervasive.

> In 2006, the Prime Minister appointed a committee headed by Shri Rajinder Sachar. This committee made a detailed study of the economic, social and educational conditions of Muslims throughout India. This report shows that Muslims are the happiest in Gujarat. Muslims receive mainstream education. Their literacy level is fast improving. The proportion of Muslims in high government services is better when compared to Uttar Pradesh or West Bengal. Economic prosperity of an average Muslim is far better than in any other State. Per capita income of Muslims in Gujarat is also highest in the country.

❑

Fastest Development in Madhya Pradesh and Chhattisgarh

Shivraj Singh Chauhan Dr. Raman Singh

Madhya Pradesh state came under the rule of BJP in the year 2004. During that period "Madhya Pradesh-GSDP growth was negative. The State government has inheritated virtually empty coffers, totally derailed economy and entirely neglected social sector.

Agricultural Growth- the Highest in the Country

Agriculture is the mainstay of Madhya Pradesh's economy. The State Government led by the Chief Minister Shivraj Singh Chouhan accorded topmost priority to make agriculture a profitable proposition by reducing its cost and increasing production as well as productivity. The committed efforts made in this direction propelled Madhya Pradesh to the top in overall food grain production for which the President conferred on it the prestigious Krishi Karman Award this year. The overall farm output in Madhya Pradesh of 142.45 lakhs MT in year 2001-03 has increased to 302.12 lakh MT in year 2011-12, representing a 112 percent increase. Madhya Pradesh has registered 18.89 percent agricultural growth rate last year, the highest in the country.

BJP rule brought a vast area under irrigation

State economy is mainly agrarian. The State Government gave top priority to increase irrigation facility. The area under irrigation was merely 7 lakh hectare in year 2003-04 against which last year 24 lakh hectare was irrigated and this year one lakh hectare more is going to be added. A number of long pending irrigation projects have been completed bringing a vast area under irrigation.

Construction and Upgradation of 90,000 KM long Roads.

Poor infrastructure has failed to leverage its immense natural and mineral wealth for all round development. Road, nine years ago, were a butt of jokes in Madhya Pradesh. But now the state is known for its reasonable good condition. Over last nine years of BJP rule more than 90,000 K M long roads have been constructed and upgraded. A sum of Rs. 1900 crores has been made available for this purpose during the period. The budget of years 2013-14 proposes Rs. 4,970 crore allocations for road sector.

Availability of Electricity to all Households and Farm Sector

Energy sector has also undergone a transformation over last nine years. Since year 2004 the state has witnessed addition of 5,033 M W in availability of electricity. Given the abysmally poor condition of energy sector nine years back, it was pipe dream to think of 24x7 availability of electricity in households and 8 - hours supply to farm sector. The state government has made possible what seemed impossible when it came to power. Since May end all rural households in the state are getting this facility. For this an ambitious feeders separation project is being executed apace.

Rapid Industrialization

Well concentrated efforts made towards accelerating the pace of industrialization have borne quite encouraging results. Despite global economic slowdown Madhya Pradesh is witnessing rapid industrialisation. About a decade ago, the prospective investors and industrialists never thought of coming to Madhya Pradesh, due to poor infrastructure. Now Madhya Pradesh has emerged as a preferred investment destination. As many as 91 major companies have started production. The industrial policy has been made more investor friendly. At the global investors summit, MOUs worth Rs 3.77 lakh crore were inked.

Special Attention to Women & Children

There has been a total shift in the approach to social sector over last nine years. The present Government conceived and implemented innovative schemes. Some of these schemes such as Ladli Laxmi, Mukhya Mantri kanyadhan, Deendayal Antyodaya Upachar, Mukhya mantri Majdoor Suraksha have been widely appreciated at national level. So far, 11.50 lakh girls have been benefited by the schemes. Chief Minister Shivraj Singh Chouhan distributes National Savings cheques to girls under the scheme at functions in districts. Under Mukhyamantri Kanyadan Yojna, launched at the initiative of Chouhan, marriages of over 2.19 lakh poor girls have been solemnised at government expenses so far. The scheme has proved to be a boon for daughters of poor families. Amount of benefit under Mukhyamantri Kanyadan Yojna has been increased from Rs 7,500 to Rs 10,000 per marriage.

Teerth Darshan Yojana

A Very special programme is launched with a spiritual mission. It takes the elders to the centers of their faith in the name of "Teerth Darshan Yojana." The scheme respects the feelings and sentiments of elders towards the pilgrimage for holy places of worship. So far One lakh elders above 60 years of age have been taken in 101 trains to the spiritual places like Rameshwaran, Kashi, Puri, Dwaraka , Vaishnodevi, Tirupati, Shirdi, Ajmer, Velankanni etc. "On the whole common people are overwhelmed by concern shown by the state government by arranging the journey of their faith.

Good Governance

To promote good governance, the state Government has

made the best possible use of information technology besides bringing in path breaking legislations like Public Services Deliverance Act and Special courts for confiscation of properties acquired by public servants through unfair means.

One would thus see that Madhya Pradesh has undergone a great change under the leadership of Chief Minister Mr. Shivaraj Singh Chouhan, making a mark in all sectors of development and welfare. The average GSDP growth during last five years has been close to 10 percent.

The last nine years have also seen an unprecedented increase in state's own tax revenue. It was merely Rs. 6,805 crore in the year 2002-03 which has increased around five fold to Rs. 33,381 crore in the year 2013-14. Madhya Pradesh has given a very good account of itself on other parameters of prudent fiscal management. Madhya Pradesh has reported revenue surplus for last nine years consecutively. The previous Government had a heavy dependence on debts against which the present Government reduced it by increasing its own resources

Madhya Pradesh has been appreciated at national and international level for the comprehensive development of all sections of society.

Chhattisgarh

Chattisgarh, a 21st century State, came into being on November 1st 2000. Larger than Tamil Nadu, it is just the right size, and is also fortunate to have a low population density. Good Governance is the highest priority in this Fast Track State. There is both policy stability as well as political stability because of the excellent rule of BJP.

Chief Minister, Dr. Raman Singh proudly says, that our focus is on two areas-good governance and good infrastructure. If we can provide these two, the rest will follow."

Farm procurement process is kept transparent in Chhattisgarh. Procurement is through co-operative societies. Middlemen and traders are completely eliminated. On the spot payments through computer generated cheques cuts out leakages. This way the government has achieved 100% paddy procurement of 71 lakh metric tonnes from 10 lakh farmers.

Chhattisgarh PDS is rated as best in the country by the Supreme Court of India as well as by the Planning Commission. It is fully computerized and ensures zero leakage and pilferage.

Chhattisgarh has led the country in guaranteeing right to food to its every citizen. Under the Act, 42 lakh families (90% of State population) are covered. In the last five years, there have been no hunger death or farmer suicides.

Chhattisgarh has achieved a zero power cut in both rural and urban areas despite the per capita electricity consumption having gone up 5 times from 300 to 1557 units. Korba is considered as the energy capital of India.

Chhattisgarh leads India in completion of projects under Pradhan Mantri Sadak Yojana - an initiative started by Vajpayee govt. - 5464 kms of roads constructed in last 8 years, investment of Rs. 8000 crore made for building rail corridors.

In Chhattisgarh, the focus is on free & compulsory education. The Govt. has built 37000 schools in last ten years, free cycle have been distributed to all girl students.

Chhattisgarh runs Swalamban Yojana to give free training to widows, divorcees & unmarried women for self employment, tools and training to Artisans for self employment.

There has been a total shift in the approach to social sector over last nine years. The present Government conceived and implemented innovative schemes. Some of these schemes such as Ladli Laxmi, Mukhya Mantri kanyadhan, Deendayal Antyodaya Upachar, Mukhya mantri Majdoor Suraksha have been widely appreciated at national level. The scheme has proved to be a boon for daughters of poor families. Amount of benefit under Mukhyamantri Kanyadan Yojna has been increased from Rs 7,500 to Rs 10,000 per marriage.

Sincere Efforts of BJP in Himachal Pradesh

When the BJP government in Himachal Pradesh was running the 3rd year, during that period I made a visit to the state and personally met many people. I am giving few important aspects of my visit.

The journey for Shimla virtually commences from Kalka Township in Panchkula District of Haryana, rightly called the gateway to Himachal Pradesh. It was Navaratri time, and there was a surge of devotees in the ancient temple of Goddess Kali, situated in the foothills of the Himalyas, causing a traffic jam in the heart of the town. Most people going to Shimla take the celebrated toy train from here that passes through more than 100 tunnels amidst a vista of stunning natural beauty. Choosing to travel by road, I had to sacrifice much of the fun. Barely had

we proceeded forward, another traffic jam awaited us. About a thousand vehicles were parked in a queue for unloading apples brought from the orchards of Himachal. These delicious delicacies were to reach the marts of Jalandhar, Chandigarh, Delhi and beyond. The State is known as the fruit basket of India; and apple constitutes 40 percent of the fruit produced in the State.

Himachal Pradesh government has assigned high priority to health, education, investment, tourism and cottage industry. It has won the national award for its outstanding performance for best enrolment under Rashtriya Swasthya Bima Yojna. In 2008, it got the national award for protecting the environment. The CM told me that his government was concentrating on development of industries, roads and power generation schemes. On being asked whether the HP "government is doing anything for the weaker section of the society, Prof. Dhumal said, social security pension to the aged, widows and physically challenged people have been enhanced by 55 per cent. This has benefitted over 2.52 lakh vulnerable persons. "We are taking special care about the development of scheduled caste and tribes of the State," he said. I also learnt that 50 per cent of the seats in Panchayats have been reserved for women.

The Himachal Government not only gives subsidy for construction of new houses to SCs/STs and OBCs, but it also helps them to repair their old houses. Keeping of cows and rearing of lambs and goats bring good remuneration to women. Loans amounting to Rs. Three lakh are made available for purchasing of cows by individual or self-help groups. Out of this 50 percent loan is interest free and even rest of 50 percent is subsidized against timely repayment of loans. Fish culture helps farmer to augment their income.

We went up to the last village on the borders of Tibet viz Kaurik. There river Sutlej just enters from Tibet at that point. On banks of that ice cold river many hamlets are bristle with activities of livestock farming. Many co-operative societies run by women have been established with the assistance of the government. They are engrossed in manufacturing woolen goods. They produce tweed wollen jackets, coats, caps, shawls, stoles, mufflers, blankets, scarves with angora and pashmina wools.

We met Smt. Sunila Sharma, an executive member of the Shikhar Handloom and Handicrafts Weavers Cooperative Society in the village of Rampur (District Kullu). More than a hundred women work with her. She showed us how the wool is sheared from lambs, sheep and rabbits. She took us to various centers where wool is processed through carding, spinning, dying, weaving, finishing, quality assurance, merchandising and finally marketing. The best thing I noticed was the confidence among the workers. They have come to enjoy monetary freedom through dignity of labour.

Himachal's tea production has not received wide renown. But its history of tea cultivation is perhaps older than that of Assam or Darjeeling. Tea cultivation in Kangra district dates back to 1849. The first commercial tea plantation began in Hailey Nagar tea estate at Holta (near Palampur) in the year 1852. Roughly 4180 hectares area stretching from Jogindernagar (District Mandi) to Shahpur (District Kangra) came under cultivation by the end of 1880. Quality of Kangra tea won gold and silver medals in Amsterdam and London markets from 1886 and 1905. But in 1905, a severe earthquake struck the region, ruining tea plantations. Panic stricken British planters sold their plantations to local people and left the country. Local people could not maintain plantations profitably due to lack of technical knowledge.

But lately an initiative has been taken by the Himachal Government, the Central government and the Tea Board revive the sick industry. To improve the quality of Kangra tea, four cooperative tea factories at Palampur, Baijnath, Bir and Sidhwari have been set up by the Himachal Government. As a result of these efforts Kangra tea is ready to be repositioned at international level. At present, the state is earning between Rs. three to five crores out of tea industry. There is scope for new plantations in non-traditional areas.

Apple is the most recognizable fruit crop of Himachal Pradesh. Apple plantation constitutes about 48 percent of total area under fruit crops. In recent years, mango has emerged as an important fruit crop. Litchi is gaining ground in certain parts of the state. Mango and Litchi are fetching better market prices. In the mid hill zone, the agro climatic conditions are optimal for successful cultivation of fruits like kiwi, olive and Strawberry. Elaborate arrangements are being made for making the packing material available to fruit growers for quality packaging.

During the course of my travel, I visited the house of Surinder Dharma of village Mohan ka Bag (Tehsil Kumarsain, distt. Shimla). Aged around 40, he is an educated farmer and a knowledgeable person. He owns an apple orchard spanning 85 bighas. There are more than 2300 plants in his orchards. The main variety of apple cultivated is Royal Delicious. He incurs an expenditure amounting to Rs seven to eight lakhs per year over maintenance of the orchard. Besides this, Rs five lakh is required for protection from heavy winds, labour, cleaning, polishing, packing, transporting to markets. Total expenditure per year is around Rs 15 lakh. The total return from his orchard ranges from Rs 20 to 25 lakhs per annum.

Agriculture is the main occupation of the people of Himachal Pradesh. It provides direct employment to 70 per cent of the population. Rice, wheat and maize constitute the important cereal crops. The BJP government has accorded top priority to agricultural production so as to increase the income of farmers. The emphasis is on production of off season vegetables, fruits and flowers. Horticulture has turned out as the most remunerative diversification of land use in the hills. Himachal has an elaborate department of Horticulture with offices spread across the State. During the last few years, the diversification programmes has brought 20,431.4 hectares under fruits, 262 hectares under flowers, and 584.3 hectares under medicinal and aromatic plant cultivation. In total 825,922 sq m has been brought under protected cultivation of horticultural crops which collectively contribute around Rs. 2,000 croe per annum towards the State GDP. The thrust is on mushroom cultivation, bee keeping, floriculture and fruit processing, etc. Horticulture acts as a money multiplier in the farming sector. With scientific farming techniques like use of poly houses and micro-irrigation more and more farmers are reaping the benefits of crop diversification.

I concluded my HP visit on a happy note. I found the BJP government making sincere efforts to secure quality life, liberty, empowerment, health and happiness for the inhabitants of the state. It is clearly visible in the expansion of employment opportunities and enhancement in the standard of living. There are many leaves one can take out of governance in Himachal Pradesh. Although temperature wise a cool state, the warmth of hospitality oozes out of it. I ended my HP tour merrily, with the blessings of Devi Shyamla, after whom Shimla is named like I had entered the state by the blessings of goddess Kalika.

During the course of my travel, I visited the house of Surinder Dharma of village Mohan ka Bag (Tehsil Kumarsain, distt. Shimla). Aged around 40, he is an educated farmer and a knowledgeable person. He owns an apple orchard spanning 85 bighas. There are more than 2300 plants in his orchards. The main variety of apple cultivated is Royal Delicious. He incurs an expenditure amounting to rupees seven to eight lakhs per year over maintenance of the orchard. Besides this, rupees five lakh is required for protection from heavy winds, labour, cleaning, polishing, packing, transporting to markets. Total expenditure per year is around Rs 15 lakh. The total return from his orchard ranges from Rs 20 to 25 lakhs per annum.

❑

Unique Electoral Strategy In Goa

Goa Legislative Assembly

Voters of Goa were preparing themselves to elect their forty colorful bunch of candidates to the Assembly on March 3, 2012. Goa people, owing to their high percentage of literacy are a politically conscious lot, compared to the other states of India. However, there has been a general disillusionment amongst the people regarding the honesty and sincerity of the politicians. Many Goans feel that better improvement and development of the State can be ensured with more involvement of dedicated people in the politics of Goa.

The battlefield was mixed with both known old faces and people who were fresh and new to politics. BJP had entered into an alliance with the Maharashtrawadi Gomantak Party as an electoral strategy to avoid the split in the anti-Congress vote. BJP was contesting in 31 constituencies, MGP in 8 and one independent was supported by both BJP as well as MGP. Congress party is fighting in 33 constituencies and remaining 7 were given to NCP.

Catholics constitute a substantial 26 per cent of the State's population of 15 lakh. The Church has played a more than a religious role in the recent past. It was involved in mass agitations directly or indirectly. It directly participated in the protests to make the Konkani language as the official language of the State. Some Congress leaders wanted to create a rift between the two tall leaders of BJP namely North Goa MP

Shripad Naik and Manohar Parrikar, leader of Opposition in the Assembly. Parrikar brushed aside the talk of rift in the party and said Shripad Naik is a senior leader of BJP. He has contributed much in building the party in the State. He will not do anything which weakens the party, he said.

Major issues

Ruling Congress suffered from strong anti-incumbency factor. It was not able to answer the public anger on issues ranging from alleged multi crore illegal mining scam to the Regional Plan 2021 and the medium of instruction of schools across the State.

Goa has been reeling under a controversy of illegal mining in which ores worth several crores were sent across the border without paying royalty or tapped by violating environmental norms. Goa's Chief Minister Digambar Kamath who had held the mining portfolio, had come under severe attack from both the BJP and his own party men over the scandal. The Public Accounts Committee headed by BJP's Manohar Parrikar, claimed the State suffered Rs 4,000 crore loss due to illegal mining.

After exposing Digambar Kamath led government on illegal mining front, Goa BJP had woven its election campaign around the raging issue, promising people to save legal mines and providing them amenities in a transparent manner through revenue earned from iron ore in legal manner. Manohar Parrikar, BJP leader said that the Congress led government had failed to come to the rescue of the people living in the mining belt. BJP had aimed to spend a major portion of the amount earned from here in infrastructure creation of the mining belt.

There was widespread anti-Congress sentiment. It was very evident that Congress was in trouble. Issues such as illegal mining, deep rooted corruption, the controversial regional plan, medium of instruction, lack of development, infighting were likely to hit the Congress Party very hard. Several Catholic leaders had joined BJP. This was an indication of prevailing atmosphere of hope and confidence.

Kamath's much touted futuristic land use policy had become another tricky election issue. The Regional Plan 2021, which was meant to deliver planning and future road map to Goa, had been opposed by the BJP, his own party men and the Church. Kamath was even accused of selling out to the real estate lobby. It was also rejected by the civil society and several panchayats in the State.

The medium of instruction in Goa schools was the major issue confronting the Congress. The move that English, along with regional languages such as Konkani or Marathi should be permitted as the medium of instruction at the primary level for aided schools, had evoked sharp reactions among the public at large. The government, at present offers aid and grants only to schools in which Konkani or Marathi is used as medium of instruction.

Expectation of people

The politics in Goa is another representation of its cultural heritage and history. After the independence from Portugese colonisers in 1961, was mainly a period of peace and stability. Initially Goa was a union territory administered by the Centre. Then it was granted Statehood in 1987. The erstwhile areas of Daman and Diu are now a separate Union Territory. When Goa became independent in 1961, there were two main political parties in the State, namely Maharashtrawadi Gomantak Party and the United Goans Democratic party. The former primarily based its electoral aspirations on the Hindus in the State while the latter was primarily based on the Christian electorate.

However, with the passage of time and the maturity in the political consciousness of the people, more national level political parties including Congress and BJP began entering the scene of Goa politics. Gradually people at the grass root level began understanding about the ideology of various political parties. Along with all round development of the country, BJP wants to preserve the national heritage and protect the national homeland without inhibiting the multiple expressions of regional, provincial and local concerns.

In the Assembly elections held in 2007, BJP fielded its candidates in 33 constituencies winning 14 of them. BJP had a vote share of 30.32 per cent, MGP has a vote share of 8.65 per cent. Congress had contested in 32 seats bagging 16 with a vote share of 32.25 per cent. The period between 1990 and 2005 saw a lot of unrest, with a quick succession of 14 governments in the narrow span of 15 years. It culminated in the imposition of President's rule in the State. Though last government survived for five years but it became a most corrupt government. People expect a stable, honest government capable of delivering good administration.

Favourable climate for BJP

Goa BJP chief Lakshmikanth Parsekar said BJP has reached lakhs of voters during party's Jan Sampark Abhiyan. According to him, people of Goa have greater faith in BJP and a favourable political climate was prevailing in Goa for the BJP to come to power.

I spoke to Shripad Naik, Manohar Parrikar, and Arti Mehra who was the prabhari of Goa. They all expressed uniformly about the favourable outcome of the election on March 3, 2012. There was widespread anti-Congress sentiment. It was quite evident that Congress was in trouble. Issues such as illegal mining, deep rooted corruption, the controversial regional plan, medium of instruction, lack of development, infighting were likely to hit the Congress party very hard.

I spoke to some of the BJP candidates namely, Shri Francis D'Souza contesting from Mapusa, Shri Rajendra Vishwanath Arlekar from Pedne, Shri Dayanand Rayu Mandrekar from Siolim, Shri Govind Parwatkar from Porvorim. They all felt that this time BJP was doing well. Fully prepared BJP was going to capitalise the prevailing anti-Congress sentiments.

Dr. Pramod Pandurang Sawant contesting from Sakhali, Shri Dattaprasad Madhukar Naik from Taleigao gave a positive note of winning the majority of seats. BJP had done the basic work of mobilising the support of common people by Jan Sampark Abhiyan, house to house visit by all candidates. We were fully alert and active to give a successful final finishing touch, they said. Several Catholic leaders had joined BJP. This was an indication of prevailing atmosphere of hope and confidence.

> Catholics constitute a substantial 26 per cent of the State's population of 15 lakh. The Church has played a more than a religious role in the recent past. It was involved in mass agitations directly or indirectly. It directly participated in the protests to make the Konkani language as the official language of the State. Recently several Catholic leaders have joined BJP. This is an indication of prevailing atmosphere of hope and confidence.

❑

BJP Emerging as a Force in Tamil Nadu

More than two lakh people attended the day long Fifth State Conference of the BJP in the temple town of Madurai on May 10, 2012. The massive turnout of people from across the State had made the Tamil Nadu unit of BJP a formidable player in State politics. In the conference, the Party focused on issues related to preserving the special features of Tamil language, literature, culture, and its greatness. It organised an exhibition on these aspects and arranged music and dance programmes at the venue.

Thiru Pon Radhakrishnan, the State President of BJP, called upon the workers to accept the challenge of becoming an alternative to the two major Dravidian parties in the State. He hoped that the conference would be a turning point in the State politics.

Leaders of the State like Shri L Ganesan, CP Radhakrishanan, H Raja and many more attacked the rule of DMK, particularly for its failure to protect the interests of Tamilians in Sri Lanka. Local issues such as bus fare revision

Tamil Nadu Legislative Assembly

BJP

and poor power supply management of the then government also came in focus. P Murlidhar Rao, National Secretary, said the party's objective was to organise the next conference in Chennai while holding the reins of power in Fort St. George. If the BJP becomes powerful in Tamil Nadu, there would not be any challenge left from divisive forces in the form of bomb threats and blasts. The State unit medical cell, guided by Dr. Rajendiran and Dr. V Aravinda Reddy organised a camp for medical check up by eminent diabetologists for one lakh people.

No Mother- Son Party

All India President Shri Nitin Gadkari came to the conference venue along with the All India Organising Secretary Shri Ram Lalji. He hoisted the party's flag at the venue of the conference and lighted the kuthuvilakku (Lamp) placed in front of the majestic Meenakshi Devi statue on the dais. He appreciated the efforts of the State president and his team of office bearers for collecting the huge gathering inside the conference hall and outside. In a thundering voice he said "Bad times for the Congress have started and the BJP led alliance was going to capture power in the next Lok Sabha elections. The country was suffering because of rising prices, growing unemployment, declining exports, corruption and poverty. This miserable situation was created by Congress led UPA-2"

He emphasised that the wrong economic policies and corruption were making people's life miserable. The BJP was working hard to set the situation right. The Vajpayee-led NDA government had envisaged a 12 per cent growth rate and had ensured 9 per cent in a short span of time. But the growth had slid to 5.5 per cent under the UPA's rule. Congress Party and its southern ally DMK did nothing to prevent the killing of Tamilians in Sri Lanka during the ethnic strife and attacks on fishermen from Tamil Nadu. Shri Gadkari highlighted that he had told in Colombo that addressing these issues was of primary importance for cordial relations between the two countries.

He made a dig at the Congress and said that the BJP was not a mother-son or father-son party. Anyone can grow up to the ranks to reach the top in our Party. Citing his own example, he said he had risen from being a grass root worker to the party chief. He charged the Congress Party for trying to conspire to create distance between the BJP and the minorities, especially the Muslims, by branding it as communal and anti-Muslim. Shri Gadkari declared that the party was away from such divisions and recalled the candidature of Dr. APJ Abdul Kalam being proposed by the Party for presidential poll earlier.

Ban on Conversions

Shri LK Advani, Smt. Sushma Swaraj and Shri Venkaiah Naidu came to the venue of conference in the afternoon session. M Venkaiah Naidu charged the UPA for failing on all fronts including economy and security. He promised to spend 60 per cent of the budgetary allocations on agriculture, if voted to power. Shri Naidu said BJP will impose 'total ban' on religious conversions besides dealing with terrorism with an 'iron hand'. He also said Ram Setu would be declared a national heritage.

Concern about Tamilians in Sri Lanka

Smt Sushma Swaraj spoke about her recent visit to Sri Lanka. The unity and integrity of Sri Lanka should be respected in the same way as that of India. She questioned as to why when Sri Lanka's respected Tamil leader R Sampanthan says that he wants Tamilians to remain in a united Sri Lanka, certain leaders in Tamil Nadu want to promote Tamil separatism in Sri Lanka. Her statement was an obvious attack on M Karunanidhi, the DMK leader who recently had said that Sri Lanka should be divided to carve out a separate state called Tamil Eelam. She also criticised both the DMK and the AIADMK for not joining them in their fact finding mission to Sri Lanka and pointed out that Sri Lanka placed no restrictions whatsoever on our meeting the people displaced by war. These people told them about all their grievances without any let or hindrance.

Huge Gathering

Senior party leader L K Advani traced the evolution of the

BJP. He said from being one of the four recognised political parties after the 1952 general elections, it had grown to become a strong alternative force to the Congress Party. He emphasised that India can become a super power only when there is a government known for good governance and that can promote welfare of the common man and ensure the security of the country in all respects. The BJP is the only party which aims to bring happiness in the life of common people and make Bharat a super power. He said, "For the first time, I am seeing such a mammoth audience, which had crossed the six digits mark. I am happy that Tamil Nadu has started to respond and support BJP so well.

Thus, the conference generated a good amount of hope and confidence in the minds of the large number of workers, admirers, supporters and the new entrants to the BJP, who had gathered to attend the Meet.

> The massive turnout of people from across the State has made the Tamil Nadu unit of BJP a formidable player in State politics. In the conference, the Party focused on issues related to preserving the special features of Tamil language, literature, culture and its greatness.

❑

Overseas Impact of BJP

MANY expatriate Indians in the United States with strong nationalist feelings had felt impelled for some time to contribute and work towards projecting a positive and correct image of India and its people. They formed the Overseas Friends of BJP (OFBJP) to work towards strengthening social bonds and to create a 'Think Tank' of intellectuals of Indian origin to foster a cordial relationship between the overseas Indian community and the American people.

Conference of Delegates

Shri Vijay Jolly (Co-Convenor, Overseas Friends of BJP) and Shri V Shanmuganathan Addl. Secretary of BJP Parliamentary Party participated in the OFBJP National Council meeting held in Chicago from July 22 – 24, 2011. Over 60 delegates across US attended the three day National Council meeting where over 200 Indian Americans attended the public function.

Dr. Adapa V Prasad, serving professor of Washington

Medical College who is the President of OFBJP, USA presided over the conference and delivered the presidential address. Shri Amar Upadhyay, an IT professional and the General Secretary of OFBJP, USA welcomed the delegates. The office bearers and delegates from all over the United States participated in the proceedings. OF BJP, USA is a vibrant and growing organisation across the USA. The organisation has five zones covering all 50 states. It has 16 chapters covering New York, New Jersey, Washington DC, Chicago, Atlanta, Detroit, Houston, San Francisco and Los Angeles.

The Indian representatives conveyed the best wishes of Shri Nitin Gadkari, All India President of BJP. Dr. Mahesh Mehta played an important role as the elderly guide and national Coordinator. People showed an immense interest in the dramatic changes occurring across the political, economic, and social landscape of India. They were appreciative of the important role being played by BJP to influence these changes in a positive manner to make India strong, secure, and prosperous.

The delegates from India explained the challenges and opportunities before the BJP. They explained as to how the BJP President Shri Gadkari gave importance for the self performance audit and workers training camps. This suggestion was taken seriously. They chalked out a programme to conduct training camps in all the five zones across the nation within a period of six months. Shri Vijay Jolly, appreciated and stressed the need to reach out to the larger Pravasi Bhartiya community and wanted the OFBJP membership and support base to be expanded in the coming months.

Contents of discussion

An overview of OFBJP's activities was presented by Shri Chandrakant Patel. He is the organising secretary of OFBJP, USA. Shri Rajendra Prasad Singh is the Vice President of OFBJP, USA. He presented the concept of Vasudhaiva-kutumbakam and the greatness of the Vedic civilisation. He narrated the unique cultural values of Bharat and how it can benefit the day-to-day life of every individual. Role of information technology and media in contemporary politics was also discussed. An

Indian -American perspective of evolving natural partnerships in the modern time at global level was also discussed.

Anecdotes from the lives of Pt. Deendayal Upadhyay and Dr. Syama Prasad Mookerjee were narrated in an inspiring manner. The general theme of the collective discussions covered subjects like working with renewed vigour, getting connected with people, involving more and more youth, building up the organisation with mutual trust and confidence.

The evening public meeting started with much fanfare at 7 pm and went on till 10 pm. It was very well attended by the admirers of BJP from the greater Chicago metropolitan area. Over 200 people attended this colourful function. The function started with the ceremonial Deep Prajwalan, Shanti Mantra and rendition of American and Indian national anthems respectively. Dr. Mahesh Mehta set the tone for the meeting by delivering a brief speech about the activities of BJP.

I spoke about the positive achievements of the BJP ruled states in India at some length highlighting India's strong commitment to democracy, justice, liberty of thought and expression, belief in equality of status and of opportunity for all. I explained how the Indian diaspora has made significant contribution towards development of many societies worldwide. While they have neatly merged with the host communities they have also retained links with their roots. I also interacted with young IT professionals in New Jersey, scientists in Washington DC and students in New York. They described the general social and economic conditions of the Americans.

Issues facing America

Americans are unhappy about their country's prospects and politician's handling of the situation. Many of them expressed their frank opinion saying that America was on the wrong track. The US Dollar was falling drastically. Incessant inflation was caused by excessive issuing of currency notes. The American culture is driven by luxury and conspicuous consumption. At the age of sixteen, the American boy or girl wants to have a car and an apartment to live. Parents were finding it difficult to keep the boys or girls with them beyond their 16 or 18 years of age.

It was very expensive and costly. One hour of tuition in English or mathematics or violin costs them 25 dollars. When parents work for more money and dollars they spend less time with children and so develop less of affection. Many parents do not communicate with their children informally. So the children are not under the control of parents. They are more under the control of hormones. At the age of 16, there are unwed mothers as pregnancies take place during school outings and excursions. How to prevent pregnancy was a lesson to be taught in the schools. Abortion is not allowed by the Catholic Church. Girls and boys choose their partners. Girls still prefer a non smoker and a non drug addict as husband. Lust and infatuation dominates the mood with only a few of them understanding what the real meaning of love and life was. Love marriages become successful if the partners complement each other without contradicting.

Ambition in life makes them hard working. It gives them stress and strain also. They have to compete with other talented people to grab the rare opportunity. On the plus side, I was impressed by a bill board in New York. When I was just moving around, the busiest Times Square in New York City, there was a big board of advertisement. It said "O! Americans! From today start thinking of "We" instead of "Me". That is the only way to get united".

Scientists and IT professionals expressed some optimistic opinions about American economy. When the Americans have felt particularly gloomy about their economy, they made special efforts to bounce back. They increased their industrial production, made new innovations through R&D, turned their growth rates high and finally conquered the inflation and stagnation. Their military might is supreme in the World. America is too big to fall.

> When I went to Washington I visited Abraham Lincoln Memorial. I was quite impressed by a carving on stone near his statue. It is written "This American Nation under God shall have a new birth of freedom and that government of the people, by the people, for the people shall not perish from the earth."

❑

Ring Side View of Parliament

Right to live with dignity

People in general are disgusted about the constant accusations, disruptions and interruptions in both the Houses of the Parliament. The Members of Parliament running to the Well of the House and shouting slogans for forcing adjournments are considered unfortunate interruptions. With such incidents occurring frequently, a serious question often asked is whether there can be a meaningful dialogue and discussion there at all? Fortunately, during the Winter Session-2011, in spite of interruptions and adjournments, several meaningful dialogues have taken place. Out of such issues, one may mention three: exploitation of the Ganga, golden jubilee of liberation of Goa and the protection of Safai Karamcharis.

Shri Arjun Ram Meghwal called the attention of the Minister of Social Justice and Empowerment to take adequate

safety measures to protect the lives of Safai Karamcharis (sewer cleaners) and provide health insurance cover to them. The BJP Member from Rajasthan raised the issue of welfare of sewage workers including their conditions of work, employers' liability, workmen's compensation and old age pension. The sewage workers and septic tank cleaners are doing remarkable work and their health and safety must be taken care of by the government. In the event of death or disablement, these workers or their dependents must be entitled to statutory compensation. It is also necessary to ensure regular health check-ups and adequate healthcare for the workers engaged in hazardous sanitation work.

While responding to the points raised by Shri Megwal, Shri Mukul Wasnik replied that as per the information received from the States, the number of manual scavenging workers is about 1, 60,000. The Union Government has started a scheme for their rehabilitation and self-employment and some State agencies have been appointed for rehabilitation of the people engaged in manual scavenging. Some Non-Governmental Organisations (NGOs) too have informed the Government that many people are still engaged in manual scavenging in some states (In some places human waste is taken out manually and cleaning of dry latrines is done physically). We brought this information to the notice of the State governments and asked them to tell the factual position after conducting an enquiry. All concerned have to fulfill their responsibility for rehabilitation of these people. It is the responsibility of the local bodies, State governments and Union Government to take steps for the safety of the sewerage workers and septic tank cleaners working with them. So far as social justice is concerned, if we are able to protect the Fundamental Rights and Right to Live with Dignity of these fellow citizens, then we can say that we have achieved that goal. If a section of our society is not living with dignity, then it means that we are not ensuring social justice for them. It is not the job of the government alone to change social circumstances, the people's representatives will have to work in that direction, and the society should become more sensitive towards them.

Ruthless exploitation of the Ganga

Shri Hukmadeo Narayan Yadav of BJP spoke in the Lok Sabha about the threat to the very existence of the river Ganga. We call the Ganga as our mother. Like the milk of the mother nourishes all parts of the body of a child, similarly the water of the Ganga nourishes our entire society. The Ganga is a boon to our crops. It is our national duty to maintain the cleanliness of the river. But the schemes and plans of the government for cleaning the river remain on papers only. All the rivers which originate from Himalayas ultimately merge in the Ganga. If these rivers remain clean then only the water of the Ganga will remain clean. Other members cutting across party line also expressed their concern about the river Ganga. A lot of illegal activities are taking place in the Himalayan region. Illegal mining is taking place and thereby causing adverse impact on our environment.

The river is more than 2,510 km long. Its basin is the largest in India, constituting over 26 per cent of the country's land mass and supporting as much as 43 per cent of its population, covering 230 cities and towns. A number of tributaries of Ganga like the Mandakini, Alaknanda, Yamuna, Kali Ganga, Ram Ganga, and the like originate in the Himalayas. The civilisation that has flourished along the banks of this great river is one of the longest surviving civilisations of the world. The river not only provides ample surface water but also keeps the underground water level recharged. The sustainer of millions of people

However, it is now under a severe threat of extinction. The disposal of huge amount of domestic and industrial waste into it all along its length is turning the river into a drain carrying all sorts of filth, poisonous chemicals and other harmful material. The Central Pollution Control Board in its recent report has said that the total coliform is a type of harmful bacteria found in foecus. count in Patna downstream has been calculated as 60 times higher than the permissible limit.

In 1996, the Supreme Court had banned the discharge of effluents from various tanneries and factories located on its banks in Kanpur (Uttar Pradesh). Nearly 50 per cent of the leather processing units in the Ganga river basin are located in Uttar Pradesh.The massive unplanned construction activity and illegal mining in and around the Ganga basin also pose danger to her banks and the pan.

Every Indian feels proud in saying that he comes from the country where Holy Ganga flows. Dumping of sewerage from urban areas and half burnt dead bodies thrown into the Ganga have turned the river into a gutter. The Maha Kumbhs are held on the banks of river Ganga. Crores of tourists, devotees and saints not only from our country but from abroad come to attend these great events. The Ganga used to flow mightily once. Its water possessed life saving medicinal value. It provided habitat to a variety of flora and fauna. But now all these living beings are facing extinction. Another problem has been added by the coming up of a chain of hydro-power generating schemes. Down from Kedarnath Dham to river Mandakini a chain of dams has been constructed despite opposition from the people of the area.

In India, the Ganga is not just a source of irrigation. Over the ages it has become the central point of faith of the common man, believed to be sacred and divine. The members jointly pleaded with the government to clean up the river, though a 'Bhagirath Prayas' in deed.

Golden Jubilee of the Liberation of Goa, Daman and Diu

It was on December 19, 1961, the Indian Armed Forces launched 'Operation Vijay' and liberated Goa, Daman and Diu from the shackles of Portugal. The House congratulated the people of Goa, Daman and Diu on the occasion of completing 50 years of freedom and conveyed its best wishes to them in their march towards prosperity and all round development.

Smt Sushma Swaraj spoke about the liberation of Goa. December 19, is celebrated as Independence Day of Goa. Not only the people of Goa but the people from other parts of the country went to Goa to join the struggle for freedom from Portugal. Sarvashri Jagannath Rao Joshi of Bharatiya Jan Sangh, Shri Madhu Limay and Jamuna Prasad Shastri from Samajwadi Party had participated in freedom movement of Goa. It may be placed on record that two very distinguished Members of the House – Prof Deshpande and Shri Tredib Choudhary had offered Satyagraha for the purpose and were incarcerated for a number of years in jail during the infamous regime of Salazar. The grateful nation granted the status and pension of freedom fighters to the people who participated in this struggle on the line of the freedom fighters of the 1947 liberation. Unfortunately, some nine people from Jammu and Kashmir who had participated in the freedom struggle of Goa were not granted pension so far even as the State Government had communicated the fact in writing. These people are very old now and a meager amount of pension was not important for them. All the same, it is needed to be recognised that they had fought for liberation of Goa.

The nation had to wait for 14 long years i.e. from August15, 1947 to December19, 1961 to get Goa, Daman and Diu liberated from the colonial yoke of Portugal so as to complete the process of Indian Independence.

> Shri Arjun Ram Meghwal called the attention of the Minister of Social Justice and Empowerment to take adequate safety measures to protect the lives of Safai Karamcharis (sewer cleaners) and provide health insurance cover to them. The BJP Member from Rajasthan raised the issue of welfare of sewage workers including their conditions of work, employers' liability, workmen's compensation and old age pension. In the event of death or disablement, these workers or their dependents must be entitled to statutory compensation. It is also necessary to ensure regular health check-ups and adequate healthcare for the workers engaged in hazardous sanitation work.

❑

Developing a Strong and Modern Armed Forces to Protect Our Borders

(Some Musings on Military Matters)

India wants to maintain good relations with her neighbours. Our armed forces are not provocative. India never tried to enter into any confrontation with any country. We always try to develop friendly relations with our neighbours. Of late, certain tensions are mounting on the borders. We cannot ignore our neighbouring country's army personnel crossing our border and making incursions. We have to be alert, ever vigilant and our armed forces must be fully prepared to face any eventuality at any time. We share a border of thousands of kilometers with China, Pakistan, Nepal and Bangladesh. The world knows that Pakistan is encouraging cross border terrorism to create tension on day-to-day basis.

Despite our long history of friendship with the people of Nepal, developments there during and after the recent elections should draw our attention. The track record of the Maiosts who have staked their claim to power in Nepal is not positive. Attacks in the past by them on Indians and Indian interests in Nepal, their leaders' open warning to India after the elections, the violation of Indian borders by their cadres give enough cause for concern.

The border between India and China is currently defined by a 4,056 km long Line of Actual Control (LAC) which is neither marked on the ground nor on mutually acceptable maps. Enormous efforts made since mid 1980s to have a recognised LAC through a Joint Working Group (JWG) of officials and experts have made little headway. China is still holding a large chunk of territory, 38,000 sq km. (14,670 sq miles), in Aksai Chin which was occupied after the 1962 blatant invasion. It claims yet more.

Another 5180 sq kms (2000 sq. miles) of area in northern Jammu and Kashmir was given by Pakistan to Beijing as price for an all weather friendship pact signed in 1963. China had already built a road through Aksai Chin linking Tibet with its Zinjiang province before it laid an aggressive claim on it. Now it seeks a political solution, not a technical one, to the border problem. The Chinese soldiers come deep into our territory in Arunachal Pradesh. There were 270 of such incursions last year alone. These troops prevent local peoples from going up to the areas where they tradionally had been taking their animals for grazing.

There was a statue of the Buddha well inside the Indian Territory. Local inhabitants used to go upto it and make their prayers and offerings. The commander of the Chinese troops had asked Indian soldiers to remove the statue. Our soldiers had pointed out that the statue was well within the Indian Territory and there was no question of removing it. The Chinese troops came and blew it off. China has developed several launching pads for air strikes at targets over land, sea and air. In this background we must be truly prepared to deal with the Chinese incursions. Simultaneously, we have to counter Pakistan's proxy war.

We need to develop a strong and modern armed force to protect our borders. Our armed forces must be ever ready to face any eventuality. We have approximately 11 lakhs Army personnel. 140 Sukhoi aircrafts are getting added to the Indian Air Force shortly. INS Jalashwa has been purchased.

Moderanisation of the Army, the Navy and the Air Force must be the top most priority. Infrastructure in the Border States must be developed on an emergency basis. Most modern roads, railway lines and air fields are necessay along the border areas in Gujarat, Rajasthan, Punjab, Jammu & Kashmir, Arunachal Pradesh, Sikkim and the States bordering Myanmar.

Our defence forces are facing several problems. There is an acute shortage of officers in all the three services. The Army is still holding obsolete Air Defence and Communication equipment, Artillery and Armour wherewhithall, weapons and spares, amunitions and other warlike stores. All such deficiencies need to be made up to manageable levels. The Air Force is much below its minimum holding of squadrons of combat aircraft. The Navy is at a low of 131 warships as against a minimum inventry of 140.

The dimensions of the modern war have not only undergone a quantum change but also have become highly resource intensive. A comprehensive defence review based on Threat Perceptions can no longer wait. As an outcome, an integrated perspective plan should be formulated which is reviewed periodically with ample room for evaluation of options and alternatives.

The Tehalka Episode and consequent accusations of kickbacks have created an undesireable degree of caution and reluctance in taking due initiatives in defence procurement deals. The problem rests with our faulty acquisition plans and opaque procurement system where a lot of reforms are urgently needed. Defence material is generally not available on the shelf. Moreover, technological advancements are so fast that in case of delay at any stage, an equipment or weapon system gets outdated by the time it actually reaches the hands of the end-user. Thus, its effectiveness or benefit gets marginalised. Defence actuations have to be planned fairly in advance factoring the gestation period and time frame of requirement into the procurement schedule. Same goes for our own production plans.

Research & Development in India constitutes a mere 6.1 per cent of the defence budget. But of this, a mere 7 to 10 per cent is spent on fundamental research whereas the bulk goes for the import of foreign technologies. Due to involvement of 'big money' the production and sale of arms is controlled by influential cartels, the world over which leave no weapon in their armoury to clinch a deal on favourable terms.A strong technological base and production capability within the country besides competent diplomacy is the only insurance against these cartels.Moreover we can not remain dependent on others for our survival kits viz. the defence equipment. We need to provide need based sophisticated weaponry to our soldiers, sailers and airmen at all levels. This is possible only when we make sufficient allocations for our own research and development in defence.

While making allocations to our defence forces, we need to consider the amount that our potential adversaries are spending on defence and their state of preparedness and capabilities. A quick look at defence spending for the year 2008-09 by Pakistan and China would show that their enhancement of capabilities is much higher than ours. Pakistan allocated 3.5 per cent of the GDP on defence by the year 2008-09, whereas China has allocated 4.3 per cent of GDP for defence. In India, in terms of GDP percentage there has been a downward trend during the last five years: from 2.14 per cent in 2004-05 to 1.99 per cent in 2008-09. In our country, a meager amount ofRs 1, 05,600 crore was allocated for defence during 2008-09.

Apart from the allocation of funds, and availability of modern weapons, the support the countrymen give more encouragement and enhances the morale of the armed forces. Our Forces are known for grit and will to succeed. Kargil was the first war victory of the Indian Arms in the full glare of television. The Battle of Monte Casino fought during the Second World War was so far known to be the toughest of the operations in mountain warfare. That claim has beene dwarfed by the Kargil actions.

> We need to provide need based sophisticated weaponry to our soldiers, sailors and airmen at all levels. This is possible only when we make sufficient allocations for our own research and development in defence.

❑

Jammu & Kashmir : Courage and Determination is the Need of the Hour

Beginning June 11, 2010, there has been an unremitting cycle of violence in the Kashmir valley, gravely threatening law and order and public peace. The violence in the state has followed a certain pattern. It is triggered through planned stone pelting by crowds targeting police stations, police outposts and other public property connected with security outfits. There were as many as 872 stone pelting incidents during June and July 2010 causing injuries to 1266 security personnel. While reacting in self defence the security forces always try to ensure that children and women are not hurt. But, when the security personnel come under fire from the instigating rogue elements they resort to counter firing under compulsion. So far 63 civilians have been killed in such incidents. It is widely known that children and women are paid Rs. 500/- per day for carrying out stone pelting operations by terrorist outfits. Some armed militants mingle with the crowds and open fire at the security forces to escalate violence.

The situation in Kashmir Valley is not normal. The present situation is the result of politics of competitive communalism practiced by both Peoples Democratic Party (PDP) and National Conference (NC). The UPA government at the Centre has taken no effective action and has been supporting both the rival parties viz.NC and PDP. Such an approach encourages the separatist elements that in turn are exploited by their masters in Pakistan.

Participating in the recent Lok Sabha discussion on August 26, Dr. M M Joshi blamed the UPA Government for 'groping in the dark' to find a solution. He cited Prime Minister's announcement that the government was ready to hold a dialogue on genuine grievances and wondered whether this meant discussion on demands for independence or autonomy. If the genuine grievance is about the demand for Independence or autonomy, then the government should tell them in unequivocal terms that these were not acceptable.

The Union Minister Farooq Abdullah has made an impassioned plea to the political class to take steps to win "the hearts and minds of the Kashmiris" to solve their problems. Taking part in a discussion in the Lok Sabha on the situation in the Kashmir Valley, the National Conference patron also made out a forceful case for reclaiming Pakistan-occupied Kashmir (PoK) and theNorthern Territories now under China's control. He said,"It is in this august House that a bill was passed several years ago asserting that the entire Jammu & Kashmir, including PoK and Northern Territories, was an integral part of India. No one is talking about the latter two regions, even though the authorities there have unleashed unparalleled atrocities on the people."

Jammu & Kashmir, maintained Shri Abdullah, had decided to merge with India because of the latter's policies and has since resolutely remained a part of India, even during the Kargil incursions. He asked those fighting for an independent Kashmir to do an honest soul-searching and find out whether it was possible for the region to remain independent for long. "China is waiting anxiously to gobble it up. Pakistan has been sending terrorists across the border to spread mayhem. It is surrounded by three nuclear powers. Can it really remain independent? Kashmir will go the Afghanistan way before long and Talibanise itself," the former J&K Chief Minister warned.

He invoked the autonomy proposal being pushed forward by his party and contended that India could thrive only if it maintained a true federal structure. "India will one day have to have a true federal set-up. If any state is weak, the Centre cannot be strong," he said. The autonomy proposal, however, evoked a mixed response. While the CPI backed it vociferously, the BJP opposed it vehemently.

With this background, the BJP MLAs from Jammu & Kashmir came to New Delhi last week and handed over a memorandum cautioning him against any dilution in the presence of security structure in J & K state. They also urged him not to succumb to the pressure of any separatist demand. For BJP, the issue of Kashmir's complete integration with India is one which the party has pursued relentlessly since its birth as Bharatiya Jana Sangh. Dr. Syama Prasad Mookerjee, the founder President of the Jana Sangh, had laid down his life for the cause of integration of the State with the motherland. Jammu and Kashmir has been culturally and historically an integral part of India from times immemorial. No power in the world can ever separate it from India.

Dr. Syama Prasad Mookerjee, the founder President of the Jana Sangh, had laid down his life for the cause of integration of the State with the motherland. Jammu and Kashmir has been culturally and historically an integral part of India from times immemorial.

❑

Indian Ethos is on Family Building not Family Breaking

Speedy Divorce Law Faces Strong Protests in Rajya Sabha

The government introduced a Bill in Rajya Sabha on 30 April, 2012, to amend the existing marriage laws to make divorce easier in case irretrievable breakdown of marriage between two consenting adults. BJP opposed the legislation on the ground that certain provisions could be dangerous for women. Not only that, other opposition parties including the SP, BSP, CPI, and CPM, besides a Congress member opposed the Bill and sought, not to reduce cooling off period for couples,

to end their marriage through divorce. In fact, all the major opposition parties accused the government that Bill was brought in hurry.

The institution of marriage is considered sacred in Hindu society. Hindu Marriage Act, Hindu Succession Act and Hindu Adoption and Maintenance Act came into existence after independence to bring equality between men and women with the aim that women should be empowered by giving rights. Many people spoke expressing a deep concern.

What will Happen to Physically or Mentally Challenged Child?

Smt. Jaya Bachchan spoke about the serious consequences of divorce. "Even today divorce is considered a stigma on our society. She has been divorced, she is wrong, she has done something bad. Our society in India is basically a middle-class society. The cooling period should not be reduced. I cannot imagine a man and a woman, who have mentally or physically challenged child, can ask for divorce. We as a State are not yet developed enough to look after such children."

Smt. Maya Singh pleaded for more cooling period. She said, "Provisions of 6 to 18 months time regarding pronouncement of decision in case of divorce has been taken away with this amendment while the Parliament Committee had opposed to abolish the provision of compulsory waiting period. Issue related to the share of wife in property earned after marriage has been left to the courts. I have doubt that women will get justice there. I request that there should be an explicit policy in this regard. Government should find out domestic, social and financial reasons behind the divorce and should try to eradicate those reasons instead of making the process of divorce simple. This will instigate divorce and it will be misused against the women. It will encourage contract marriage."

Bill is against Vulnerable Section of the Society

Shri Tapan Kumar Sen expressed a deep concern about the weaker section. He said "This Bill is a reflection of biased mindset against the weaker and the vulnerable section of the society. I stress on the proportional sharing of marital property because when women mostly get separated, they are separated with children. So, the children's account also have to be taken into account while sharing of the marital property. In many cases, while making assessment of the marital property, it has to be ensured that the real income of the household property is disclosed. It should not be just left to the discretion and understanding of the court as such. It must be ensured that a provision is made for women and children to have a house and a place of residence. The laws relating to the maintenance for women and children must be strengthened to ensure that women and children receive an adequate amount of maintenance which will be sufficient for them to live a lifestyle. There should be some special arrangement so that the women facing a divorce should not face the legal hazards they normally face."

Dowry is Major Reason for Divorce

Shri Ram Kripal Yadav opined that marriage is considered a sacred in our society. Shri Yadav said "Practice of dowry is major reason behind the divorce. Despite our efforts, practice of dowry still exists in our society. Our society doesn't consider divorce a good thing. Divorce is accepted always as last option when it became inevitable. Life of women become miserable after divorce as we are male-dominated country and in most of the cases male is source of income. Safety of future of children borne out of marriage should be ensured. We don't want the cases of divorce increase. We are going to simplify the process of divorce in haste. It should be reconsidered. It needs to be checked. No one prefers divorce but after this amendment trend of divorce will increase and will make an ill effect on society. I request that it should be reconsidered. We should not enact any such law which will promote divorce. This Bill should be brought only after intense considerations. As it is a sensitive Bill so don't bring this in any such haste."

Family System will be Destroyed

Shri M. Rama Jois stated that this amendment together with 1976 Amendment, providing for divorce by consent, encourages divorces, which is injurious to the children and family. "The relationship brought about between a man and woman as husband and wife through marriage is irreversible. Just because husband and wife have divorced each other, what would happen to the children? Who is going to bring them up? Therefore, such legislations are injurious to the national interest and should be given up. A matter of this magnitude, which affects the entire society, must be considered coolly. If the husband and wife do not talk to each other, does that mean it is irretrievably broken down? Therefore, the present legislation, which increases the desire to get divorce, is ultimately ruinous to our society. In the entire world, this family system of India, is appreciated. We are, completely, destroying this spirit, and we are being influenced by sex and lust. We must reverse this stand."

Women are always the Sufferer

Dr. Najma A. Heptulla said that "The Indian ethos is on family building, not family breaking. That is why the thought of divorce was unthinkable in Indian society. Today time has changed. Women are asserting themselves. In Islam not only men but women can also go for divorce. Unfortunately, the women never do it and they are always the sufferer. The Bill has a provision which allows both the parties to file for a divorce on the ground of irretrievable breakdown of marriage. Both the parties have to live apart for, at least, three years before filling such a petition. This can be misused. The wife has a right to oppose the grant of a divorce on the ground that dissolution of marriage will result in grave financial hardship to her. The court shall consider all circumstances including the conduct of the party, children, before deciding whether a divorce would result in hardship. We cannot make laws in India according to the Western society where social set up is different from ours. The Standing Committee has recommended that the six months' cooling period should remain. I also feel so. I don't think there is anything which is really irretrievable. I am happy that you are bringing an amendment regarding adopted children. When two people get married, they become the owners of the property. But there is no system in our country that the wife becomes co-owner of her husband's property. You have to take care of that. This law is not going to be only for educated urban women but for uneducated rural women also. We should relook into the irretrievable breakdown of marriage and take the recommendation of the Standing Committee more seriously."

Don't Do Injustice to Women

The Leader of the Opposition, Shri Arun Jaitley asserted that "Conventionally, divorce in India is granted either with consent or granted to a party which is suffering from a matrimonial default caused by the other party. The simple principle being that no person can take a benefit of his own default to get a divorce. I think, if we start with such a legislative policy we will be doing a great injustice to the women."

Finally, speedy divorce got delayed with a proposed amendment to the Hindu Marriage Act, 1955. It was stalled in Rajya Sabha. Law Minister Salman Khurshid, referred the Bill to a select committee of Parliament, sought time to respond to the Bill, leaving the Bill's fate hanging.

Shri Tapan Kumar Sen expressed a deep concern about the weaker section. He said "This Bill is a reflection of biased mindset against the weaker and the vulnerable section of the society. I stress on the proportional sharing of marital property because when women mostly get separated, they are separated with children. So, the children's account will also have to be taken into account while sharing of the marital property.

❑

Parliament on Plight of Hindus in Pakistan

UPA Government fails to address the issue

Recently, in separate incidents, three Hindu girls in the Sindh province of Pakistan were reportedly abducted, forcibly converted to Islam and married off against their will to Muslim men. Hindus living in Pakistan are not only facing undue harassment, their cultural, religious and human rights are also being openly violated. The BJP Parliamentary Party discussed the plight of Hindus in Pakistan which has forced many of them to flee to India, and decided to demand a debate on the issue in both the Houses. The aim was to impress upon the

government to take the matter seriously.

On 2.5.2012 during the zero hour, Dr. Murli Manohar Joshi raised the issue concerning the Hindus in Pakistan. He spoke about the reported violations of Human Rights in respect of Hindus in Pakistan, particularly in Sindh. The issue was taken up in Rajya Sabha as well. The Minister of External Affairs, Shri S M Krishna assured that he would personally convey the concerns of the House and of the people of India to government of Pakistan. This has become a worrisome aspect of deliberations in Lok Sabha and Rajya Sabha because talking frankly about the problems of Hindus is considered as communal. Due to this atmosphere many MPs don't raise the problems of Hindus at all. The following report of discussion in Parliament thus becomes an important event of this session.

Issue of cultural and Human Rights

"The kind of incidents taking place in our neigbouring country Pakistan are complete violation of Human and cultural rights of Hindus. I feel sad that our Prime Minister did not raise this issue when he met the President of Pakistan. Our Foreign Minister also did not raise this issue. And the current situation in Pakistan is that young Hindu girls are abducted and forcibly converted to Islam. Even after the court's order they are not given protection. There, young Hindu girls are identified and kidnapped and then raped and forcibly converted to Islam. More than 400 Hindu families have migrated from Sindh to India in the last 10 months. It is unfortunate that Home Ministry and Ministry of External Affairs are completely silent on the issue and are not taking it seriously. When Ministry of External Affairs was asked about it they said that it is Pakistan's internal matter. Issue of human and cultural rights is not an internal matter."

"It is laughable that people of Delhi are not aware, how many Hindus have come here as refugees from Pakistan. Home Minister is sitting here. These Hindus have not migrated on account of smuggling. They have come here for the protection of their cultural and human rights and because of the atrocities of Pakistan authorities.

We should not forget that Pakistan is a theocratic state. That is why minorities are being tortured there. We have very big and strong Human Rights Commission in our country and we cannot tolerate these atrocities on Hindus. But all this is happening in our neighbourhood and the government is silent on the subject. When they come here they complain that they had faith on the Indian government they will protect their cultural and human rights but this government is betraying us and it is not protecting us. This news is circulating in the papers for so many days but no action has been taken for the protection of Hindus in Pakistan. I want to know from the government that when Pakistan's President visited India, 'was this issue raised before him?' This is a serious question What message are we giving to our countrymen? What message are we giving to international community? Are we telling the world that India is not willing to fight for the cultural and human rights of the Hindus in the world? We have always been advocating for the safety of human and cultural rights but what is happening to Pakistani Hindus is genocide. Hindus are being forced to evacuate Pakistan simply because their culture is different from Muslims. Finally they will come to India because they cannot go anywhere else. They cannot go to Arabian Sea neither to Afghanistan. What is the duty of Indian Prime Minister, Foreign and Home Ministers? India wants an answer to this. Will you give protection to them? Will you speak to Pakistan's government to stop all such atrocities on Hindus? Will you raise this issue at International Human Rights Commission? Will you give assurance to Indians that any religion originating from India will be protected?"

"I want to remind you that when India was divided we advised Hindus to stay back in Pakistan as the Indian government is here to protect them. During that period 15 per cent Hindus were there but now it has come down to 2 per cent. What is all this? For how long will we tolerate this type of cultural genocide? We want to know from the Central Government what their policy on the subject is? What protections are they planning for these helpless families? This is genocide of cultural rights, an invasion of a particular religion and culture by a government through deliberate policy? Can you accept all this? We cannot accept. Therefore we demand from Prime Minister, Foreign and Home Minister to assure the nation about 'what steps will they take to avoid repetition of any such atrocities on Hindus in future?' This is not a communal issue but of cultural and human rights for which India only can take responsibility to safeguard them. I feel sad that Indian government kept quiet for so long and did not raise its voice over the plight of these unfortunate people. Is it crime that they are Hindus?"

The same issue was taken up in the Rajya Sabha. Some of the members of Rajya Sabha spoke about the problem in depth.

Call the High Commissioner of Pakistan

Shri Husain Dalwai (Cong) : "Today, whatever is happening in Pakistan is not only serious but also against the humanity. This is the situation that women are not safe there. Girls are abducted and are forced to marry. They are converted. That is why many of non Muslim families are migrating in India. After migration to India those who live in camps, their condition is also very bad. But our Government does not pay proper attention towards them. The High Commissioner of Pakistan should be called and be asked as to what is happening there? The Hindu here is liberal. He stands with us. The people know that justice is here. I think that the Government should strongly tell that if it is not stopped, we would raise this question at International Forum."

All Party delegation of MPs should go to Pakistan

Shri Avinash Rai Khanna : "Atrocities are being committed against minorities in Pakistan. They are forced to accept Islam. They have to give ransom to be alive. Girls of minority community are kidnapped and forcibly converted to Islam. After that they are married to Muslim men. On oppositing they are threatened to be killed. Human Rights are being violated in Pakistan but it is a matter of sorrow that there is no reaction from the Government of India. I would like to say that an all-party delegation should go to Pakistan and see how minorities are being treated there. They should be encouraged and assured that India is with them. Rules of giving citizenship should be simplified and the victims of atrocities in Pakistan who come to India should be cordially treated."

Safety of Minorities and their rights in Pakistan

The External Affairs Minister (Shri SM Krishna) : "There is an imperative need for us to live as good neighbours. That is possible only when Pakistan subscribes to this concept of 'good neighbourly relationship'. There is nothing like one handed clap. It is imperative for Pakistan to fulfill its commitment of not allowing its territory to be controlled or to be used for fomenting terrorism against India. In the last few years, it has come to our notice that forces which are hostile are going scot-free in Pakistan and carrying on a hate-India-campaign. We have conveyed to Pakistan that this is not going to help in bettering India-Pakistan relations. Treatment of minorities in Pakistan is a matter of grave concern to the people of India. We have also seen the reports of encroachment of places of religious worship in Pakistan. It is the responsibility of the Government of Pakistan to discharge its Constitutional obligations towards its citizens including those from the minority community. The Government has understood the sense of the House. When I take up the issue of protection and safety of the minorities and their rights, I can certainly take up the question of religious places and its plights in Pakistan also."

Give citizenship to Hindu Refugees

Shri Balbir K Punj : "In 1947 when we got independence, country was divided in two parts and this Partition was based on religion. Pakistan declared itself as an Islamic nation, but we did not do that. We adopted a secular Constitution and we are proud that system of democratic and secular Constitution is doing well for the last 65 years. In 1947 the population of Hindus and Sikhs in Pakistan was 15 per cent and in the census of 1951 it was 11 and 12 per cent.

Today the number of 11-12 per cent Hindus and Sikhs has come down to 1.4 or 1.5. Hindus and Sikhs were insulted and forced to take refuge in India or they were forcibly converted. The official report of national Human Rights Commission of Pakistan contains that every month 25-30 such cases appear in Government record that Hindu girls are taken forcibly. After that they are converted and are married forcibly. They are made Muslim. The judges are also afraid there. This House and Parliament avoid discussing the human rights of Hindus in Pakistan. People, who came from there, were managed but today we don't care for the people who were left there believing leaders of this country. There cannot be a bigger deception than this. The Hon. Minister should assure that visa would be issued to the refugees, Hindus coming from Pakistan without any difficulty. The Hindus who want to take refuge here should immediately be given citizenship of India."

> "The kind of incidents taking place in our neigbouring country Pakistan are complete violation of Human and cultural rights of Hindus. There, young Hindu girls are identified and kidnapped and then raped and forcibly converted to Islam. More than 400 Hindu families have migrated from Sindh to India in the last 10 months. It is unfortunate that Home Ministry and Ministry of External Affairs are completely silent on the issue and are not taking it seriously. When Ministry of External Affairs was asked about it they said that it is Pakistan's internal matter. Issue of human and cultural rights is not an internal matter."

❑

UPA-II Clueless While Prices Go Sky High

The Government admits that market prices of essential commodities have gone up: rice by 20 per cent, edible oil by 40 per cent, milk products by 12 per cent, potato by 12.5 per cent, wheat by 8.3 per cent and atta by 7 per cent. This is an alarming state of sky-high price rise. Similarly, the prices of almost all other essential commodities like sugar, pulses, red chlli, gram, fruits, vegetables, drugs and medicines have risen massively.

The inflation is not just 7.4 per cent. It is much more. People are forced to spend more money for food than for other purposes. The rural poor spend 55 per cent of their income on food items alone. The urban poor spend 45 per cent of their income on food. Then, how can they meet expenses on education, health, housing, clothing, and transport etc. This situation is causing serious distress to the middle class, lower middle class and poorer sections of the people. The UPA Government is going to leave behind a chronic inflation. Although inflation affects all the classes, the poor are hit the worst. Not only will their incomes fall but their sources of income may disappear altogether.

The Prime Minister says that it is difficult to stop inflation. Another minister says that there is no magic wand to stop it.

That it is a natural consequence of rapid economic growth opines another. They should understand that China has made rapid economic growth for the last two decades but its inflation currently is below two per cent. There is a Tamil proverb which says if we have sufficient stock in the pot or in a container then only a spoon can take more food out to serve. Otherwise how could it be possible?

Economic Survey Report of the Finance Ministry says that the years 2001 and 2003 witnessed high levels of stock build up in the central pool. The foodgrain stocks reached a peak of 64.7 million tonnes, an all time high record. On the other hand, in January 2008 the actual stock was only 7.7 million tonnes, which was lower than even the buffer norms.

Last year our farmers produced 93 million tonnes of rice, 75 million tonnes of wheat, and 14 million tonnes of pulses, in spite of many odds, difficulties and suffering. But the Food Corporation of India could procure only 35 per cent of its proposed target. A substantial percentage of foodgrains produced in our country is cornered by certain corporate sector for profiteering at a later stage. If we were self-sufficient in food, oil or other essential commodities, surely we would not be worried of what was happening in the world. But, we are importing 70 per cent of our crude oil requirement besides huge quantities of edible oil and pulses. The high oil prices impact agricultural costs directly because of significance of energy as an input in the cultivation process itself. In the last few years, the crude oil prices have increased from $37.7 to $112 a barrel. In the same way, palm oil prices have soared from $471 MT to $622 a MT.

Unfortunately, there has been a neglignence in the field of agriculture, right from the beginning of economic reforms of1991. Capital formation on agriculture was reduced. There is an utter mismatch between supply and demand. The growth in agricultural production has come down to less than 2 per cent. In one year, it was 1.87 per cent less than the growth in population. This has happened because of neglect of agriculture in our country. During the last 4 years, 8 million hectares of agricultural land where foodgrains were grown has shifted to other cultivation. Farmers prefer to grow cash crops such as sugarcane, cardamom, jute and cotton. But the real truth is that more and more farmers want to leave the sector itself. How long can they continue to suffer? So, farmers have left villages. Due to this development production of cereals, especially wheat, pulses and oil seeds, has been going down over the last few years. This is the real cause of discontent among the masses.

The shortage of food is one important problem that needs to be addressed through a long-term strategy combined with short-term measures. A number of suggestions are made by agricultural scientists to increase production through innovative methods and by achieving breakthrough in managing water, seeds and fertilizers.

This is very clear that if we want to bring down the prices and curtain inflation, increasing productivity in the agricultural sector is the only way. Moreover, proper attention needs to be given to the Public Distribution System. In sum, what is required is a massive and effective governmental intervention to ensure that the poorest Indian gets food and other basic necessities of life in adequate quantities at affordable rates.

> The UPA Government is going to leave behind a chronic inflation. Although inflation affects all the classes, the poor are hit the worst. Not only will their incomes fall but their sources of income may disappear altogether.

❑

Congress Misusing CBI for Political Bargains

The Central Bureau of Investigation (CBI) has become a political arm of the ruling Congress party. The CBI has been used as a threat to corner the Opposition leaders and get their support to serve the political interests of the ruling party. There is indeed a vulnerable section in the Opposition. It is vulnerable because of cases of corruption against their leaders. CBI was utilised to defeat the cut motion in the Parliament. Now the CBI is being used to harass senior leaders of the NDA and other Opposition leaders.

Unfortunately, ordinary people of our country are carried away by the silent, serious, thoughtful face of Congress PM Manmohan Singh. Behind this innocent appearance, a blatant misuse of the Central Bureau of Investigation is going on unabatedly. People in general must understand as to how the UPA Government has destroyed the independence and autonomy of the CBI. Some examples:

1. The Bofors case is systematically finished by misusing the CBI. The Italian businessman Ottavio Quattrocchi no

longer figures in the CBI list of wanted persons and has removed the 12 years old Interpol red corner notice against the lone surviving suspect in the Bofors pay-off case.

2. Congress leader Jagdish Tyler accused in the 1984 anti-Sikh riots case was given a clean chit by closure of case against him.
3. The case against Ajit Jogi for attempting to buy MLAs was cleverly finished.
4. Sanction for prosecution was not granted against Satish Sharma in a case of nepotism regarding allotment of petrol pumps.
5. The case of possessing disproportionate assets against Lalu Yadav was weakened by changing the public prosecutor. A special bench of the Income Tax Appellate Tribunal was created to exonerate him of any tax liability and legitimise his wealth so that it can be used as the basis for acquittal in the criminal trial. When that did happen, the CBI was advised not to file an appeal before the High Court. When the State Government filed an appeal, the CBI took the plea that nobody else had the authority to go for an appeal.
6. The case against the BSP leader Ms Mayawati regarding the Taj Corridor was diluted when the BSP support was required in 2007. However, at the time of no confidence vote in 2008 the case of disproportionate assets against her was activated when she was actively opposing the UPA. Suddenly in April 2010, a statement was made before the Supreme Court seeking to dilute the case of disproportionate assets against Mayawati, when her support was required in the voting for Cut Motion in the Lok Sabha.
7. Affidavits in the case of Mulayam Singh Yadav were changed depending on the circumstances when he supported the Government or when he opposed it.
8. A false case against Shri George Fernandes was registered in relation to defence transactions, even though the Commission of Inquiry headed by Justice Phukan had

categorically opined that there was no case against him.

9. Today the State of Gujarat is witnessing the tyranny of the CBI with a systematic effort made to harass the functionaries of the State government, particularly Police officers, in order to intimidate them and take vindictive action against them. This is being done in cases which have already been investigated by the Special Investigative Team set up by the Supreme Court.

During the last six years, the UPA government has failed in controlling prices of essential commodities. It has not been able to handle the Maoist violence and check the attacks of terrorists. Its ministers are involved in serious corruption charges. The allocation of 2 G spectrum by the Telecommunication Ministry at throw away prices to a chosen few has caused immense loss to the public exchequer. But ironically the Congress is successful in using CBI to cover-up the crimes of the leaders of the UPA by subverting or closing the cases. The UPA Government led by Congress coerces the vulnerable leaders of Opposition parties by misusing the Central Bureau of Investigation. By using this ever hanging sword they are brought to the bargaining counter so as to muster a parliamentary majority. The ruling Congress directs the CBI through the government to act in a vindictive manner in the cases related to strong opponents of the UPA. People should fight this abuse of power on all forums and find justice.

The UPA Government led by Congress coerces the vulnerable leaders of Opposition parties by misusing the Central Bureau of Investigation. By using this ever hanging sword they are brought to the bargaining counter so as to muster a parliamentary majority.

❑

Social & Cultural Background

Social Equality & Harmony

Tribute to Dr. B R Ambedkar on 120th Birth Anniversary

A team of RSS karyakartas went to a village called Madappally in North Arcot district of Tamil Nadu some years ago. During that time I was Prant Pracharak of Tamil Nadu. The local Dravida Kazhagam leader was invited to preside over the annual celebration of the shakha. He was a non-believer and local president of Dravida Kazhagam (DK) which was working for social justice. It was a pleasant surprise to all when he accepted the invitation and came to the function.

More surprise awaited us, when at the close of the function he went back and brought sweets for distribution. He explained, "In fact, a few days ago I had come here with the intention of opposing you and stopping your activities since all of our DK workers were upset about your starting Sangh work in our village. But when I saw that boys of the agrahram (Brahmin Locality) and those from the Harijan Mohalla were freely mingling and playing together with joy and enthusiasm and behaving just as the children of a single family, I was totally disarmed. I felt our founder, Periyar EV Ramaswamy Naicker too had dreamt exactly of a similar casteless society. The dreams of great social reformers like Dr. Ambedkar and Periyar EV Ramaswamy Naicker are fulfilled by your Sangh. You have silently succeeded in realising their dreams. Hence I offer my good wishes and sweets to you."

It is natural that such a powerful movement for social

harmony and unity generated by thousands of shakhas spread all over the country should have a strong ideological foundation. RSS is working hard to organise the Hindu society. Organising means bringing the people together and making them realise the purpose for which or values for which they are living together. This is not an easy task. There should be an emotional basis of our unity. Hindustan is our motherland. We are the children of this great 'Bharat Mata'. We have been living together for the past thousands of years and have created a glorious history. Our contribution to the world's thought, culture and civilisation is a well known fact.

RSS makes an honest appeal that we being the children of this soil, must come together and live together. It is essential to feel that we are all one and that we are all equals. At the same time we should also be able to experience this oneness in our day-to-day life.

The history of India tells us that a handful of Muslims and Englishmen could rule over us by exploiting the differences among our people. They could forcibly convert our brethren to their religions. Dr. Hedgewar, the founder of RSS, used to say that we cannot escape our responsibility by simply blaming the Muslims and the Europeans for our downfall. We have to admit that social inequality amongst us has been one reason for our downfall. Fissiparous tendencies like caste and sub-caste rivalries have all been the manifestation of social inequality. This evil must be rooted out.

Social inequality still is a saddening and unfortunate aspect of our society. Some intellectuals express their opinion as it was non-existent in the olden times, but at some stage during the passage of time, it entered into our social system. According to the late Balasaheb Deoras, the third Sarsanghachalak of RSS, "Untouchability is a terrible folly and it must be thrown out lock, stock and barrel. There are no two opinions about it. Abraham Lincoln, who abolished slavery in America, had said if slavery is not wrong, then nothing is wrong. Similarly, it is for all of us to declare, if untouchability is not wrong then nothing in the world is wrong."

RSS explains to the people at large how our society became weak and disorganised on account of social inequalities. RSS tries to eradicate social inequality in each and every form. The second Sarsanghchalak Sri Guruji had brought together all the religious leaders on a common platform under the auspices of Vishwa Hindu Parishad to persuade them to this viewpoint. As a result, many saints and religious leaders have commenced mixing amongst all sections of society. They have given up their previous opposition to reconversion and come forward to take back into their fold those brethren of ours who had been converted.

Unfortunately, there are some people in our society who believe in discrimination and are unable to grasp the right attitude. They are also part of our Hindu society. It is not necessary that we should denounce such people and teach them in a hard way. There are certainly other ways of persuading and bringing them together. Sri Bachharaj Vyas was a swayamsevak in Nagpur. Having born in a highly orthodox family, he had difficulties in meeting and mixing with various sections of people. When he first attended a Sangh camp, taking meals with some people posed a problem for him. He could not eat meals prepared and served for all. When Dr. Hedgewar came to know about the problem, he did not quote any rule of the camp and prevent Shri Bachharaj Vyas from attending the camp, since he was certain that the desired reformation would definitely take place in him. He knew Shri Bachharaj was a man of great caliber and selfless at heart. He allowed him to attend the camp with his own utensils and ration. Shri Bachharaj cooked his food himself and ate it all alone. That was the first year. The next year, Shri Bachharaj himself told Dr. Hedgewar, "I shall take meals with the rest". Thereafter, as he involved himself more and more in Sangh work his behaviour underwent a metamorphic change in spite of his orthodox background. He became a trusted worker of the Sangh and served as the provincial organiser in Rajasthan. Later, he even became all India president of Bharatiya Jan Sangh. This was the way Dr Hedgewar worked.

It is a fact that the backward or dalit brothers of ours underwent a huge amount of humiliation, misery, insults and injustice for centuries. That agony is there in their hearts. Everyone is pained at this sight. Such a behaviour with them is wrong and it should stop forthwith. Oppressed brethren are also part and parcel of our own Hindu society and we have to ensure a dignified living for them with other members of society.

The RSS constantly makes appeal to all the people to stand shoulder to shoulder with others who have similar ideas and feelings, and then the combined efforts of all makes the task much easier and brings the goal much nearer. Working for the economic and political betterment of those who had been relegated to the background and bringing them up to stand shoulder to shoulder with all the rest of our people are a Herculean tasks. Strenuous work springing from the heart and manifesting itself in day-to-day behaviour, work on a spiritual, moral and social plane is also needed.

The RSS and its various organisations conduct programmes like bhajans, keertans, festivals, recital of stories from Ramayana and Mahabharata. Local people assemble in the spirit of common brotherhood submerging all differences in an environment of pure dharmic devotion. Service projects promoting literacy, health, employment, sports etc are also undertaken on a big scale. The central point of RSS inspired activities is the personal appeal to the heart, the emphasis on the unifying and ennobling factors, and ignoring of differences.

Babasaheb Ambedkar presided over the Makarsankranti utsav of Pune Shakha in 1936. There he asked Dr. Hedgewar, who was present at the ceremony, whether all members of RSS were Brahmins. Dr. Hedgewar's answer was that when swayamsevaks were spreading their ideals and recruiting new members that is using their brain they were brahmins, when they were performing their daily exercises, they were kshatriyas, whenever they handled money and other business matters for the Sangh, they were vaishyas, and when they did the sanitation work in their various camps and branches, they were shudras. In other words, by naming the four main traditional castes into which Hindu society is divided Dr. Hedgewar made the point that the RSS was attempting to demonstrate that caste meant nothing. Dr. Ambedkar was very much impressed with such castlessness in the centre of orthodoxy in Maharashtra.

Mahatma Gandhi, while addressing the RSS workers in Delhi in 1947, remembered that during his visit to an RSS camp years ago he had been 'very well impressed by their discipline, complete absence of untouchability and rigorous simplicity."

All this was achieved not by any sermons but by daily examples. Non existence of caste differences within the Sangh has been a *fact* ever since RSS was born in 1925.

> Dr. Hedgewar, the founder of RSS, used to say that we cannot escape our responsibility by simply blaming the Muslims and the Europeans for our downfall. We have to admit that social inequality amongst us has been one reason for our downfall. Fissiparous tendencies like caste and sub-caste rivalries have all been the manifestation of social inequality. This evil must be rooted out.

❑

Noble Deeds Turn Foes into Friends
—A True Story of Incident in Nataraja Temple at Chidambaram

TEMPLES as sacred religious places symbolize the core of Spiritual Bharat and are of great cultural significance. Immense sacrifices have been made by the people of the land to protect and preserve these holy shrines.

Whenever we hear the name of Golden Temple, we think of the beautiful Harmandir Sahib in Amritsar. There however is another Golden Temple in South India viz. the great Nataraja Temple at Chidambaram in Tamil Nadu which is associated with the cosmic dance of Bhagwan Nataraja. Chidambaram Nataraja temple complex is spread over 40 acres of land in the heart of the city. It is an ancient and historic temple dedicated to Lord Shiva, who gives darshan to His devotees in the form

of Nataraja. As the temple has a separate sannidhi for Bhagwan Govindaraja Perumal, it stands as a testimony for the oneness of Shiva and Vishnu. It is one of the very few temples where both the Shaivite and the Vaishnavite forms of the Almighty are enshrined at one place.

The archayas (priests) of the temple are called Dhikshitars. They have been taking care of this temple since it came into existence. They are called as Thillai Moovaayiranaar (3000 families of priests of Thillai). The Dikshitars are respected by the devotees as Bhagwan Shiva himself. They are well versed in recitation of the Vedas and Sanskrit shlokas and are also masters of Tamil hymns such as Thevaram and Thiruvachakam, etc. There are thousands of Tamil Thevarams, sung by Nayanmars and other saints. The Dikshitars recite Thevaram and Thiruvachakam also as part of the daily rituals.

Unfortunately some atheistic and alien forces conspired against the Dikshitars lately and created a controversy as though they were not singing Tamil hymns and that they also were not allowing other devotees to sing the same inside the temple.

Actually, Tamil Thevarams and Vedas are not different. Nayanmar Trio of Appar, Sundarar and Sambandar sang thousands of hymns called Thevaram while Saint Manickavachakar had composed the Thiruvachakam. The Nayanmars have depicted the beautiful Sanskrit and Tamil languages as the manifestation of Bhagwan Shiva himself. They take the bhaktas to a higher level of consciousness and wisdom by showering great spiritual thoughts through these languages. Tamil hymns worship Shiva, as the lord of Vedas. But some mischievous people created difference beyond limits. Naturally the devotees of Bhagwan Nataraja got worried. The temples are considered as centres of unity, bringing different sections of society together by organizing a variety of functions and festivals. How to bring solace, unity and amity among the community was the main question before all devotees.

At that time Shri Sudhakar, organising secretary of Hindu Temple Protection Committee, approached all groups of people and requested them to come to the temple. Hundreds of devotees, mainly youths, women and students of Annamalai

University came in large numbers and gathered in the temple premises. Shri Sabesan, secretary of RSS, explained the significance of the Temple. He said, "Chidambaram is one of the Panchabhoota Sthalas signifying the five elements of cosmos such as air, water, fire, earth and space. The famous Tamil saints like Sambandar, Appar, Sundarar and Manickkavachakar have sung verses in praise of Bhagwan Nataraja. Main significance of Chidambaram Nataraja is Ananda Thandava, (Dance of Bliss), in the Golden Hall as Sabhapathy. Nataraja is the manifestation of Shiva. His body represents the space. His three eyes symbolise the sun, moon and the eight directions and His damaru is the creator of sound. This temple is centre of unity. So we have to develop cooperation and cohesion."

Shri Ranganathan alias Pattu, treasurer of the Temple Protection Committee spoke about the philosophy behind the Temple. He said, "The world is the embodiment of the Virat Purusha, the colossal human form. Chidambaram is the centre of this form, the place of the heart, where Shiva performs the cosmic dance. Many scholars and thinkers have written about the uniqueness of the Temple. Ananda K Coomaraswamy, who originally hails from Sri Lanka but now is settled in America, has written numerous articles about the significance of the Chidambaram. He has narrated rhythm, beauty, power and grace of Nataraja. It is the clearest image of the activity of God which any art or religion can boast of.

Dr. Fritsof Capra, the author of the Tao of Physics, has explained in his book that "the metaphor of the cosmic dance unifies ancient mythology, religious art and modern physics. The importance of this temple is seen, appreciated and realised by the whole world. Today, we are here mainly to clean the complete temple with five prakaras or circuits. When we work, let us think about unity. We are all devotees of Ananda Nataraja. The power of God exists in every one of us. Let us forget our differences. Let us work together."

Then all the devotees started cleaning the temple. Most of the dirt and waste were collected and kept in a corner of the temple. It looked like a small mountain by noon time. The Dhikshitars brought food for them and served it with affection. In the evening the municipal chairman came with two tractors and arranged to remove all the dirt, dried plants, stones and other wastes out of the temple. The whole town was happy when they saw the temple completely neat and clean. They were all the more happy when they saw the worshippers working together and taking food together forgetting all their petty differences.

The archayas (priests) of the temple are called Dhikshitars. They have been taking care of this temple since it came into existence. They are well versed in recitation of the Vedas and Sanskrit shlokas and are also masters of Tamil hymns such as Thevaram and Thiruvachakam, etc. There are thousands of Tamil Thevarams, sung by Nayanmars and other saints. The Dikshitars recite Thevaram and Thiruvachakam also as part of the daily rituals.

❑

Cultural Confluence of Music and Spirituality in Tamil Nadu

During the winter season each year large religious gatherings take place in Tamil Nadu spontaneously. For instance, on December 23, 2010, more than 5 lakh devotees were blessed to witness the Ananda Thandava Shri Nataraja in Chidambaram Temple, during Arudhra Darshan. More than 7 lakh devotees had had the darshans of Ranganatha Swamy in Srirangam when Swarga Vasal (gateway to heaven) was opened on the day of Karthigai Deepam corresponding to December 17, 2010. Lately, about 25 lakh Hindus had the darshans of Arunachaleshwar and made a parikrama of the mountain inThiruvannamalai.

Karthigeya temple in Palani, attracts lakhs of devotees with kavadi on Thaipoosm day. There is no doubt that, Ayappa in Sabarimalai would be worshiped by more than five crore people by the middle of January 2011, during the Makar Sankranti festival. Here most of the devotees are men. Very few women visit this shrine. On the other hand, the Adi Parashakti temple in Melmaruvathur, near Chennai, attracts women devotees in large numbers. These are some of the largest religious gatherings found anywhere in the world where the devotees come to pray to the lord for blessings. Such annual festivals are central to the South Indian religious traditions.

SpiritualityArousesInteres

Apart from this, there are big congregations seeking

spiritual knowledge. Mata Amritanandamayi's devotees come together in lakhs to have the healing touch of the Amma. The devotees of Sri Sri Ravi Shankar Maharaj assemble in large numbers to learn about the Art of Living. He is working for a stress-free and violence-free society. Sadguru Jaggi Vasudev too attracts large crowds. He presents powerful methods of self-transformation to people from all walks of life. Swamy Paramarthananda takes spiritual classes about scriptures and shastras in a brilliant way. His teachings touch upon various aspects of life like Atman, self-inquiry, right attitude and right action and so are very inspiring.

These are the wonderful assemblies of people who want to discover the essence and meaning of their lives. They come to realise the great contribution made by our forefathers towards passing down the values of life, generations after generations, by personally practicing the principles of true ethics as propounded in our sacred lore. The participants are taken to higher levels of consciousness by astute masters through meditation, prayer and contemplation. Such unique experiences lead them to believe that spiritual practices are the foundations of happiness.

Musical Extravaganza

During the winter season of the year, sandwiched between autumn and spring, a melodious music and dance festival takes place in Chennai, the capital of Tamil Nadu. It is a grand celebration of classical music and dances of south India. Popularly known as Carnatic Music festival, it is held from mid December to mid January. The festival is held at a number of venues around the city organized by various sabhas or organisations. Performances in the festival include vocal & instrumental music and Bharatnatyam ; solo and group both by junior and senior artists. Even upcoming artists get a chance to perform along with well-established artists. The music includes songs in various south Indian languages like Tamil, Telugu, Kannada and Malayalam.

Musical instuments like the flute, veena (a large string instrument), gottuvadyam (similar to veena, but without frets), nadaswaram (pipe), thavil (a percussion instrument), mridangam (drum) and even ghatam (mud pot) are used. These musical sessions go on till mid January when the scene shifts to Thiruvaiyaru to celebrate the birth of Saint Thyagaraja, one of the greatest Carnatic composers. This annual festival nourishes the classical tradition of music. It is an ancient and sophisticated art stretching back over thousands of years, originating from temples and believed to be performed by divine artists. These classical styles are closely associated with mythology, philosophy and spiritual thoughts of the Hindu culture.

Madras city comes alive with 'Margazli Festival of Dance and Music' which has become an annual feature with thousands of artists and lakhs of people participating in the spectacular cultural event.

Production of Art Films

The Tamil Film Industry has opened up a new page in the history of Indian cinema. According to reports in the media, as many as 150 films have been produced in Chennai in the year 2010, a number which was never achieved in the history of Tamil Cinema. Rajnikanth has emerged as a super star. Recently, he acted in a science-fiction film involving a robot. It was realeased in Tamil, Hindi and Telugu versions, running very well in all the languages. According to reports, the cost of production of Rajni's Robot was about Rs 180 crores and the overall collection was more than Rs 800 crores. It is a Himalayan achievement beating all the old box office hits.

The movie Pazhassi Raja has been acclaimed as an art film in Malayalam as well as in Tamil. The story of Pazhassi Raja, one of our earlier freedom fighters was popularly known as the Lion of Kerala. The making of this grand epic film is really an achievement. It educates the younger generation about the freedom struggle through a popular medium.

Aham Brahmasmi

The whole world knows that superstar Rajnikanth often goes to Himalayas and stays there in a serene atmosphere. He associates himself with sadhus, saints and sanyasis and meditates in the vicinity of the river Ganga. Tamil language has always been rich in literature and music. But its cinema was mostly meant for entertainment. There were many who tried for a change. Among the new generation of film makers, Bala leads the pack in bringing a change in Tamil cinema's outlook and approach. He is trying hard to give a new thought to Tamil cinema. Recently, Bala has made a film called, Aham Brahmasmi, Nan Kadavul in Tamil. This creation has fetched him the national award for the best director. Naan Kadavul, Aham Brahmasmin—is a film based upon a Tamil novel namely Yelavathu Ulagam (the 7th world), written by Jayamohan who also has penned the dialogue for the film.

Much more is yet to come

Tamil Nadu is peculiar in its own way. Once, there were quite a few films with rational ideas. Some of those films were anti-God and anti-Hindu also. But, MG Ramachandran (MGR), the mentor of J. Jayalalithaa, changed the trend. He openly associated himself with the Devi Mookambiga Mandir in Karnataka. Also, the well known actor Vijayakanth appears in public with full vibudhai on his forehead. After receiving the Oscar Award in America, music composer AR Rahman declared that the credit for his achievements does not go to him, but all glory belongs to God Himself. Thus, the trends are changing. In general, people are talented, creative and hard working, making sincere efforts for excellence. Still, there is a longing for something great to happen.

> These are the wonderful assemblies of people who want to discover the essence and meaning of their lives. They come to realise the great contribution made by our forefathers towards passing down the values of life, generations after generations, by personally practicing the principles of true ethics as propounded in our sacred lore. The participants are taken to higher levels of consciousness by astute masters through meditation, prayer and contemplation. Such unique experiences lead them to believe that spiritual practices are the foundations of happiness.

❑

Vivekananda House in Chennai— A Source of Inspiration

Swamy Vivekananda House known as Vivekanandar Illam in Tamil, stands majestically on the busy Kamarajar Salai, in the marina beach, very much nearer to seashore. Swami Vivekananda stayed here for nine days between 6 February 1897 to 14 February 1897, after his triumphant return from the west. Swamy Vivekananda landed at Colombo on the afternoon of January 15, 1897 and was given a right royal reception by the Hindu community there. Then he visited Rameswaram Temple, Pamban, Ramnad, Paramakudi, Manamadurai, Shivaganga, Madurai, Kumbakonam and then Swamiji reahed Chennai.

Welcome Address in Madras

When Swamy Vivekananda arrived at Madras, an address of welcome was presented to him by the Madras reception committee. In the railway station, there was a huge audience surging with emotion to see the glimpse of Swamyji. Most hearty welcome address was read out by the devotees. It said, "When you undertook to represent Hinduism at the Parliament of religions, most of us felt, that the cause of Hinduism would be ably upheld by its representative in that memorable religious assembly. Your representation of the doctrines of Hinduism at once clear, correct, and authoritative, not only produced a remarkable impression at the Parliament of Religions itself, but also led a number of men and women even in foreign lands to realize that out of the fountain of Indian spirituality refreshing draughts of immortal life and love may be taken so as to bring about a larger, fuller and holier evolution of humanity than has yet been witnessed on this globe of ours. 'After the welcome address was over, Swamij was requested to sit on a decorated chariot. Owing to the intense enthusiasm of the large crowd assembled to welcome him, Swamiji was only able to give a short reply.' The wonderful kindness, the fervent and enthusiastic joy with which I have been received from Colombo to Madras, and seem likely to be received all over India, have passed even my most sanguine expectations; but that only makes me glad, for it proves the assertion which I have made again and again in the past that as each nation has one ideal as its vitality, as each nation has one particular groove which is to become its own, so religion is the peculiarity of the growth of the Indian mind. In other parts of the world, religion is one of the many considerations, in fact it is a minor occupation. Here in India, it is religion that forms the very core of the national heart. It is the backbone, the bed-rock, the foundation upon which the national edifice has been built. Politics, power and even intellect form a secondary consideration here. Religion, therefore, is the one consideration in India."

What Makes One Nation to Survive?

At this stage, the joy of enthusiasm of the crowd became more intense and it was a challenge to manage them. Swamiji raised his voice shortened his speech. "I do not know whether my voice will reach all of you. I never before had an opportunity of addressing a large open-air meeting." Then Swamiji continued his speech, "Two great problems are being decided by the nations of the world. India has taken up one side and the rest of the world has taken the other side. And the problem is this.: Who is to survive? What makes one nation to survive and others die? Should love survive or hatred, should enjoyment survive or renunciation, should matter survive or the spirit, in the struggle of life? Our solution is renunciation, fearlessness and love; these are fittest to survive. Giving up the senses makes a nation survive. As a proof of this, here is history, today telling us of mushroom nations rising and falling, almost every century—starting up from nothingness, making vicious play for a few days and then melting. This big, gigantic race which had to grapple with some of the greatest problems of misfortunes, dangers, and vicissitudes such as never fell upon the head of any other nation of the world, survives because it has taken the side of renunciation; for without renunciation how can there be religion?' Then Swamiji concluded his speech, pleased at the people's warmth and show of tremendous enthusiasm. It was indeed a marvelous show of strength of people ready to follow the thoughts of Swamiji Vivekananda. Then Swamiji was taken to Vivekananda house earlier known as ice house or castle kernan at Chennai.

History of the Building

This building was originally used by the British to store ice brought from great lakes in north America for about 30 years. Then this building was sold to one Mr. Biligiri Iyangar of Madras who was a famous advocate in the Madras High Court and was fairly well to do in those times. He remodeled the house, renamed it castle Kernan after his friend, Justice Kernan in the Madras High Court and used it as a residence. Biligiri Iyangar , being a disciple of Swami Vivekananda, made him stay at the ice house. Later When Vivekananda was about to depart, he agreed to his disciples request to set up a permanent centre at the ice house.

Jayalalitha Government's Gift

In 1963, during the birth centenary of Swami Vivekananda, the Government of Tamil Nadu renamed the Castle Kernan as 'Vivekananda house'. In 1997, on the eve of the centenary of Swamiji's return to India and his stay at this house, the Government of Tamil Nadu at the request of the Ramakrishna Math leased out the Vivekananda house for few years. In the 150th year of Swami Vivekananda's birth anniversary, the Ramakrishna Mission in Chennai has got a gift from the Jayalalitha Government. The state has extended the lease on Vivekananda house on the marina by 99 years, i.e. till 2111.

Experience Vivekanada

The Vivekananda house structure is distinctive and has several unique features. This is reflected clearly in its distinct architectural features such as the circular core, the semicircular corridors, the hemispherical dome and the square plan. 43 paintings of exquisite artistry trace the evolution of our culture from vedic times to the advent of Sri Ramakrishna. These paintings are colourful commentaries on the secret of the longevity of our culture. They illustrate the reach and range of India's spiritual heritage. The Vedas, the Epics, and the Puranas come alive in these paintings. The large circular verandah exhibits 120 photographs relating to Swamiji from his days as a travelling monk to his spiritual conquest of the West, which has become a part of world history. Rare photos are on display, elegantly laminated, with sub-titles and footnotes. Swami Vivekanada's room is on the second floor that Swamiji stayed in February 1897. This room, full of sacred memories is now maintained as a meditation room. Anyone who sits here even for a few minutes cannot but feel the peaceful understanding of the power of God. Meditation can be done here comfortably seated. Sri Ramakrishna Math conducts lot of spiritual programmes to experience Vivekananda. Thus, Vivekananda house is inspiring because of his personal stay. It is also interesting not only for the displays on the famous 'wandering monk' but also for the semicircular structure in which it is housed. In centuries to come, Swami Vivekanada will be remembered as one of the main moulders of the modern world.

<u>What Makes One Nation to Survive?</u>

Who is to survive? What makes one nation to survive and others die? Should love survive or hatred, should enjoyment survive or renunciation, should matter survive or the spirit, in the struggle of life? Our solution is renunciation, fearlessness and love; these are fittest to survive. Giving up the senses makes a nation survive.

❑

World Tamil Conference Promotes Sangam Classics

The first World Classical Tamil Conference was held at Coimbatore from June 23 to 27, 2010 in a grand manner. As many as 3000 delegates from 50 countries presented their research papers about the uniqueness and antiquity of the Tamil language, culture, art and society. More than 2.4 lakhs people visited the venue on the concluding day. The Exhibition Hall, Tamil Internet IT Hall, the main pandal for the conference and the food courts remained jam-packed.

There was a grand pageantry at World Tamil Meet. An eight-kilometer stretch of the pageant was titled as "Iniyavai Naarpathu" or "Sweet Forty". The three-hour procession of tableaux was part of the inauguration of the conference. The floats provided vivid images of the achievements of the Tamil people, right from literary excellence, to economic strength, love, friendship, devotion, valour, love for nature, unity, architecture, pioneering in the shipping trade, the bravery of the women, the sacrifice of revolutionary warriors, the contribution of farmers and an emphasis on environmental protection were among the 40 themes presented by the floats. The aim was to highlight the greatness and special features of Tamil Language. In terms of sheer numbers of participants and papers, this meet exceeded the eight world Tamil conferences held between 1966 and 1995.

The World Classicism in literature refers to the elements of universality, harmony, art of antiquity, style or content such as reason, clarity, order, restrain, humanitarian outlook. Some facts :

- The Tamil language has a long literary antiquity of about 3000 years.
- It has a body of ancient literature meeting the core attributes of classicism and is held as a valuable heritage bequeathed to humanity.
- The literary tradition is original and not borrowed from another speech community.
- The classical language and literature being distinct and modern it has its own glamour values. So, there was a world wide consensus that Tamil possessed greater merits for being declared as a classical language.

President Shrimati Pratibha Devi Singh Patil hailed the Tamil language as classical since it possessed the oldest literature among the living languages of the World. She said that the Tirukkural written by Thiruvalluvar was a remarkable treatise on ethics. Silapathikaram and Manimekalai were works of excellence as were the epics of Kamba Ramayana, Jeevaka Chintamani and the soul - stirring hymns of Nayanmars and Alvars.

The poems and songs of Subramanya Bharati evoked in the minds of the people deep feelings of patriotism during our freedom struggle". She emphasized a point that the history of the Tamils is our nation's pride. Tamils have contributed in a big way to India's progress and in shaping its identity as a nation that is rich in art, music, architecture and literature. The next generation of Tamils must anchor as well as 'equip themselves with knowledge of Tamil culture, literature and values.

Iravatham Mahadevan, an IAS Officer (Retd), an epigraphist and a Tamil scholar says, "The legend that Sanskrit and Tamil emerged from the two sides of the damaru (drum) of Shiva says it all - the immemorial antiquity and the equal divine status accorded in our tradition to the two languages now recognised as classical.

M. Karunanidhi delivered the valedictory address of the five day conference. He said a fund amounting to Rs. 100 crore would be established for Tamil Development. The CM said efforts would be made for translating well known Tamil works into other languages. Significant works of other languages would also be translated into Tamil. Shri Pranab Mukherjee who presided over the valedictory function expressed the hope that the conference would inspire many more accomplishments in future.

Fortunately, the DMK and its leaders kept their atheism and anti-god feelings away from the Conference hall. Really, Tamil language is full of patriotism, national culture and spiritual feelings.

The Tamil language has a long literary antiquity of about 3000 years.

- It has a body of ancient literature meeting the core attributes of classicism and is held as a valuable heritage bequeathed to humanity.
- The literary tradition is original and not borrowed from another speech community.
- The classical language and literature being distinct and modern it has its own glamour values. So, there was a world wide consensus that Tamil possessed greater merits for being declared as a classical language.

Jayamohan : A Game Changer in the Contemporary Tamil Literature

The contemporary Tamil literary world is rich with great writers and creative thinkers like Jayakanthan, Ashoka Mitran, Prabhanchan, Melanmai Ponnusamy and many more. Through their novels, short stories, poems and essays, they have created wonderful feelings and brought new ideas and fresh thoughts. They touch people's hearts by writing about their agonies, anxieties and aspirations. Many of them write about the prevailing social conditions and happenings in the day-to-day life like love, hatred, conflicts, controversies and blossoming of best qualities in human relationships.

Some writers have taken up matters like superstitions, casteism, dowry and other social evils. Earlier, many Tamil writers were propagating leftist theories or atheistic view points in the name of progressive trends and were highly critical of the Hindu spiritual thoughts. A very few writers wrote about the core Indian values. A modern Tamil writer from Kanyakumari district, Jeyamohan has presented India's rich literary and classical traditions in a majestic manner. With his original ideas and continuous writing, he has created the biggest impact on the modern Tamil literary landscape.

Vishnupuram

Jeyamohan's most appreciated work is 'Vishnupuram'. This novel carries the readers on an interesting journey. It is a fantasy set as a quest through various schools of Indian philosophy and history. Before writing this novel he took a tour of the entire country. During the centenary year of Pt. Jawaharlal Nehru,

Indian Railways gave a concession for one whole year enabling a person to travel anywhere in India in any train. Jeyamohan did not take even a single pie along with him, except a pair of clothes to wear. He had problems for food initially for a few days. Later, in the whole journey he never suffered starvation because every temple and Gurudwara served him food. He slept in railway stations, temples and choultries. He studied the life of ordinary Indians, interacted with scholarly people and made observations about the impact of our great culture on the day to day life of the common man.

During the tour, he visited Pandaripuram. After the darshan and food he slept in the corridor outside the temple. During his deep sleep he had a dream. He saw a golden river. On the banks of the river many artists and sculptors were carving stones and wooden planks thereby making idols. Then he got up and started thinking about the heritage of our country and her culture. That became the seed for his novel 'Vishnupuram' situated on the banks of his imaginary River Sona. In 1993, Jeyamohan met Guru Nitya Chaitanya Yati in Ooty near Coimbatore. It was the turning point in his spiritual journey. The dialogues with the Guru gave him a new vision. Those sacred and divine perceptions made him to write 'Vishnupuram'.

Jeyamohan's prolific contributions includes 9 novels, 10 volumes of short stories, 13 literary criticisms, 5 biographies of writers, 6 introductions to Indian and Western literature, 3 volumes on Hindu and Christian philosophies and numerous other translations and collections.

Some of his famous novels include Rubber, Pin Thodarum Nizhaun Kural, Kanyakumari, Kaadu, Panimanithian, Eashaam Ulagam and Kotravai. He had close interactions with Communists in Kanyakumari. One of his relative was a card-holder in Communist Party. There were a lot of discussions about the intolerant attitude of Stalin towards Trotsky and his close associates. Trotsky was deported from Russia and later eliminated in Mexico. Then, Jeyamohan wrote a novel, "The voice of a following shadow" – Pin Thodarum Nizhaun Kural. This novel resonates with audiences even today with its incisive analysis of self-appointed destiny makers and the movements that they create.

Award Winning Novel

'Rubber' was the first published novel of Jeyamohan. It portrays the transition of a farmer's mindset in Kanyakumari district. From times immemorial Kanyakumari is famous for cultivation of bananas. The banana plants are a natural home for birds. Banana plant is useful to the villagers from roots to the top leaves and fruits. But the farmers shifted the cultivation from banana to rubber for the sake of earning more money. Birds don't go and sit on rubber trees. Rubber is made by cutting the trunk of the tree. It was the first major work in Tamil Nadu that explored ecological and environmental degradation in the State. It is written as a multi-generational family drama taking place against the backdrop of rubber plantation. The novel describes the hunger for social and commercial growth that inevitably exploits the environment. Rubber, introduced into India as a cash crop, is the alien specie that chokes the land and destroys the values symbolised by the traditional banana. In a subtle way he communicates, "How western culture is overpowering the Indian value system". The novel won the Akhilan Memorial Prize in 1990 heralding the arrival of Jeyamohan on the Indian literary scene.

His writings are heavily influenced by spiritural persons and by the works of humanitarian thinkers like Leo Tolstoy and Mahatma Gandhi. Jeyamohan is conducting literary conferences and writers' conclaves in the Southern part of Tamil Nadu at places like Kutraalam, Ooty and Thirparappu in Kanyakumari district. Such discussions and exchanges of ideas with scholars, poets and creative thinkers gave him special and unique place in the contemporary Tamil literary world.

Screenplay Writing

Tamil film industry is always associated with popular writers. He has written screen-plays for Tamil movies viz. Kasthuri Maan, and Vasantha Balan's Angadi Theru. Famous film director Bala took his novel Ezaham Ulagam for a film called

'Ahambrahmsin' alais, Naan Kaadavul. It described the horrifying experiences of poor beggars intending to create sympathy and pity about their sufferings. He has described how mercilessly and forcibly their organs are cut or deshaped or chopped off while still young. This film got a National Award. Then he wrote the script for a Malayalam film dubbed in Tamil called 'Pazhasi Raja'. This film is about the life of a freedom fighter from Kerala.

Jeyamohan.in

Jeyamohan had been an active participant in Tamil internet discussion groups during the early years of the medium in India. As part of the debates, Jeyamohan produced some of his best essays on literary standards and criticisms during this period. Recognising the possibility of losing some of these important works, Jeyamohan's fans' circle created a literary website to consolidate the author's works. Over the decade, www.jeyamohan.in website has become an important repository of the author's essays. Jeyamohan registers his contributions extensively on his website, with more than 10,000 entries on topics ranging from Indian literature to commentary on contemporary India. Jeyamohan uses his website to continuously engage in a dialogue with his audience and develops new ideas by active association and participation of all.

More significantly, the website allows the author to freely engage in discussions with thousands of readers. In early 2011, the Vishnupuram Ilakkiya Vattam (Vishnupuram literary circle) created an online discussion group for discussing literature, criticism, art and related topics.

Son of Visalakshi Amma

Jeyamohan was born on April 22, 1962 to S Baguleyan Pillai and B Visalakshi Amma in Arumanai, near Kanyakumari in Tamilnadu. Baguleyan Pillai was an accounts clerk in the Arumanai registrar's office. Visalakshi Amma hailed from a family of intellectuals and trade-unionists - Jeyamohan considered her equal to Saraswati in knowledge and wisdom. Jeyamohan's siblings comprise an elder brother and a younger sister. Jeyamohan's younger days were spent in voracious reading and in absorbing the richness of the culture around him. His first publication during schooldays was in Ratnabala, a children's magazine, followed by a host of pieces in popular weeklies.

After high-school, Jeyamohan was pressured by his father into studying commerce at the Pioneer Kumarasamy College in Nagercoil. It was a period of tremendous inner-conflict and depression, and the suicide of his childhood friend Radhakrishnan finally drove him to leave home on spiritual quests. He sought to become a Sanyasi and travelled to the holy places of India, like Benares, Tiruvannamalai and Palani. Supporting himself through odd-jobs and living the life of an ascetic wanderer, he was constantly on the move internally and externally.

Expeditions and Explorations

Jeyamohan continued his frequent travels throughout India as a common man, in order to sustain the integrity of his narrative style and to gain intimate knowledge of the fabric that kept the nation together despite the vastness of its size and differences in culture. He is one of the few authors who have travelled and witnessed regional conflicts, droughts and political problems like Naxalism in tribal areas. His experiences convinced him of the continuing relevance of Gandhian idealism and non-violence as the sensible alternative to naked capitalism and militant socialism.

True Literature

Thus Jeyamohan has established a unique way of writing with words that capture the imagination of the reader by powerful language. It is not elaborate. His style is influenced by post modernism. Jeyamohan's ascetic like experience is an asset and has largely influenced his perception. His spiritual ideas are a combination of scientific interpretations and social values of historical scriptures. His writings on Hindu traditional values are considered significant by many. Personally, I am very much inspired by reading his articles on Kamba Ramayanam,

Thirukural, Bhagwad Gita, Sankhya Yoga, and Vedantic philosophy. Spirituality is always woven in Tamil literature. Jeyamohan wants to renew the same at an hour when literature is dominated by secular and temporal writings. True literature must echo eternal values of Indian life. Jeyamohan has done exactly that.

Earlier, many Tamil writers were propagating leftist theories or atheistic view points in the name of progressive trends and were highly critical of the Hindu spiritual thoughts. A very few writers wrote about the core Indian values. A modern Tamil writer from Kanyakumari district, Jeyamohan has presented India's rich literary and classical traditions in a majestic manner. With his original ideas and continuous writing, he has created the biggest impact on the modern Tamil literary field.

❑

The Roots

Bhagwad Gita—The Heart and Soul of Indian Civilisation

Government of India declares in Parliament

A case against Bhagwad Gita is being fought presently in a court in of the Russian Federation. Some anti-Hindu elements are seeking a ban on the great treatise across Russia branding it as an extremist literature. The case was instituted in June 2011 asking for a ban on the Russian translation of the book written by Bhaktivedanta Swami Prabhupada, the founder of International Society of Krishna Consciousness (ISKCON). It also wants the Hindu religious text banned in Russia and declared as literature spreading social discord. Indians settled in Russia and the followers of ISKCON religious movement have appealed to the Government of India and the Prime Minister to intervene and find a solution to this problem.

Intolerant Attitude of the Orthodox Church

The aforesaid case is based on religious bias and intolerance shown by some religious groups in Russia. The court case in the Siberian city of Tomsk is an attempt by the Russian Orthodox Church to place restrictions on the activities of the Hare Krishna movement, calling it a totalitarian sect. Earlier this year, the authorities banned the construction of an ISKCON Community Village in the Tomsk region. Seven years ago, the Moscow city government did not allow the Movement to build a sprawling prayer-cum-cultural complex in central Moscow. Later, ISKCON was permitted to set up its centre in Siberia.

Protest by BJP, BJD, Shiv Sena, RJD, SP and BSP

With this as background, the entire Parliament took up the issue. It was raised by a senior BJD leader Shri Bhartruhari Mahtab through a special mention stating that 'the religious rights of Hindus in Russia should be protected.' Earlier, the State Prosecutor in Tomsk had referred the Scripture to the Tomsk State University for obtaining expert opinion. The University is not qualified to render scholarly comments as it has no Indologists on its faculty who have studied history, culture, languages and literature of the Indian subcontinent.

Speaking on the occasion in the Parliament the inimitable Lalu Prasad Yadav said that insulting the Gita is insulting Krishna. Terming it as a big conspiracy against Lord Krishna, Shri Lalu Yadav demanded a discussion and a stern action. Dr. Murli Manohar Joshi and Dr. Harin Pathak supported the contention and voiced serious concerns. Uproarious scenes were witnessed when members across the party lines demanded a discussion. The Speaker had to adjourn the House time and again with a promise to allow the discussion.

Rising to the occasion Shri Mulayam Singh Yadav called the Gita a universal book accepted as such the world over. The treatise guides people to be better human beings and to work for the good of the society, he said. It is a classic that teaches honesty and how to lead a sacred life. Mahatma Gandhi used to read Gita daily and most of his speeches were based on the teachings of Gita. Gandhi Ji wanted to build the nation on the message of the Gita. But the government, said Shri Yadav, has not taken Gita seriously. Let all parties accept this fact. The Government has not taken any step to propagate

Gita amongst the people of this nation.

Many others pleaded to the government in the Parliament to take steps for teaching Gita from the primary classes to the university level. Once this happens, the dream of Mahatma Gandhi would be realised and the people would understand and practice the core message of Gita and thereby make India a better nation.

Shri Hukumdev Narain Yadav said the Government of India should seek clarification from the Russian Government on the subject. Dr. Murali Manohar Joshi said amid interruptions, that "Gita is a sovereign scripture. The Prime Minister has just returned from Russia and we would like to request him to tell us whether he raised this matter with the Russian government." The BJP, Shiv Sena, RJD, BSP, Samajwadi Party and even some members of the Congress Party sought an immediate intervention by the Government. Smt. Sushma Swaraj demanded that the Bhagwad Gita be declared as National Book.

Statement of External Affairs Minister, Shri SM Krishna

In his statement Shri Krishna said, "I fully share the sentiments expressed by the Hon'ble Members of the House on this issue.

Hon'ble Members referred to media reports about a hearing conducted by a Court in the Russian city of Tomsk on whether a Russian language commentary on the Bhagwad Gita qualifies as "extremist" literature. I would like to inform this august House of the facts of this case. ISKCON conveyed to our Embassy that its branch in Tomsk, Eastern Siberia, had received a notice in June 2011, of a complaint filed by the Public Prosecutor's Office in the local court. This complaint, apparently driven by some local individuals, was to the effect that the third Russian edition of the publication Bhagwad Gita As It Is—a translation of a commentary by Swami Prabhupada, founder of ISKCON - had certain portions that were 'objectionable' and 'extremist' in nature.

Officials of the Embassy of India in Moscow and our Ambassador have been in regular touch with the local representatives of ISKCON, since this matter came to light in June 2011. ISKCON representatives were advised to take legal recourse to counter this misdirected complaint. We have also taken up this matter at the senior levels of the Russian Government. The Ministry of External Affairs has been in regular touch with our Embassy in Moscow on this issue. The matter was also taken up with the Russian Ambassador based in India, H.E. Mr. Alexander Kadakin is himself a well-known Indologist. In fact the Ambassador has been publicly critical of this episode. He has stated that "Bhagavad Gita is a great source of wisdom for the people of India and the world." He also said that "Russia is a secular and democratic country where all religions enjoy equal respect."

"Hon'ble Members would agree that the Bhagwad Gita is not simply a religious text; it is one of the defining treatises of Indian thought and describes the very soul of our great civilisation. The Gita is far above any cheap propaganda or attacks by the ignorant or the misdirected. In Russia itself, we have many great Indologists, scholars and experts who understand the essence of the Gita and have written on it with reverence and passion. We do not want to dignify with too much attention some misdirected individuals who have filed an absurd complaint. We are confident that our Russian friends, who understand our civilisational values and cultural sensitivities, will resolve this matter appropriately."

The Gita may be considered as Rashtriya Dharma Shastra. Says the High Court

The Allahabad High Court expressed the view that it was the duty of the State to recognize Bhagwad Gita as Rashtriya Dharma Shastra, which has inspired our national struggle for freedom and also all walks of life. As India has recognised the national flag, national bird, national anthem and national flower, the Bhagwad Gita may also be considered as the Rashtriya Dharma Shastra. It is the duty of every citizen of India under Article 51A of the Constitution of India irrespective of caste, creed or religion to follow the dharma propounded by the BhagwadGita.

This view was expressed by Justice SN Srivastava while deciding on a writ petition filed by Shri Shyamal Ranjan Mukherjee, priest of the Gopal Thakur Mandir of Varanasi, challenging the sale of temple properties.

> Rising to the occasion Shri Mulayam Singh Yadav called the Gita a universal book accepted as such the world over. The treatise guides people to be better human beings and to work for the good of the society, he said. It is a classic that teaches honesty and how to lead a sacred life. Mahatma Gandhi used to read Gita daily and most of his speeches were based on the teachings of Gita. Gandhi Ji wanted to build the nation on the message of the Gita. But the government, said Shri Yadav, has not taken Gita seriously. Let all parties accept this fact. The Government has not taken any step to propagate Gita amongst the people of this nation.

❑

Greatness of Thirukkural—Ethical Pratice in Every Aspect of Human Life

The State Government of Tamil Nadu celebrates the 15th of January as Thiruvalluvar Day, as part of the Pongal (Sangranthi) celebrations in his honor. Thiruvalluvar was a celebrated Tamil Poet and Philosopher whose contribution to Tamil Literature is the Thirukkural, a work on Ethics. He is called Deiva Pulavar, that means Divine Poet. Thirukkural is one of the most revered ancient works in the Tamil language. The historical fact known about him is that he was living the life of a householder with his wife, Vasuki, following the profession of a weaver, in Mylapore, originally a part of Chennai City. A story about the wife of Thiruvalluvar, is still popularly prevalent in the villages of Tamil Nadu. While doing some important work, Thiruvalluvar called his wife who was then drawing water from well. Leaving the vessel dangling halfway down the well, Vasuki promptly rushed to answer her husband's call. The immense wonder was that the vessel remained in its dangling position unaffected by gravity, till she returned back after performing her duty. This is sure proof of her honesty by the grace of divinity.

Content of Kural

Thirukkural is a collection of 1330 Tamil couplets organized into 133 chapters. Each chapter has a specific subject ranging from "ploughing a piece of the Land" to "ruling a country". It preaches simplicity and truth throughout its verses. The 1330 couplets are arranged into three main sections and 133 chapters. Each chapter contains 10 couplets.

Thirukkural is neither a scripture nor an epic, but an extraordinary treatise on the art of living, which delves deep into the unshifting foundations of human life. Thirukkural attempts to provide guidelines, not for the society in general but for the individuals: the ascetic, the family member, the father, mother, the son, the monarch, the minister, the ambassador and in general to the individuals in society with responsibilities to themselves and others.

How should a man live? What are the virtues to be practiced by him and what the code of conduct? What the duties of the various Ashramas in which man's life falls? How should a king rule his people and protect them? What is the code of conduct prescribed for him? How can best be got out of domestic life? These and similar questions have been admirably answered in this beautiful work.

ETHICS - In Day To Day Life

Thirukkural occupies a place of pride in the classical Tamil Literature. It is respected by the Tamils in much the same way as the Vedas and the Gita, in Sanskrit works. Three of the four purusharthas that mankind should strive for, namely Dharma, Artha and Kama are dealt with at great length in his work under the names of Arathupal (Duty), Porutpal (wealth) and Kamathupal (Love and happiness) respectively. The fourth purushartha, namely Moksha has not been treated separately. It may be because at the beginning of Arthupal, Moksha is dealt with in an indirect way. To him who follows the principles at righteousness and thereby earns his living and gets his legitimates desires fulfilled, salvation is assured. There are many commentaries on his work, ten of them being very ancient, Parimelazhagar's commentary is the most famous of them. Every scholar depends on it for a correct interpretation of the kural. The special merit of this commentary is the exhibition of his erudition in the different branches of Sanskrit Learning, Tarka, Vyakarana, Mimansa and Vedanta. It is clear from the following fundamental noble ides referred to by Thiruvalluvar that he had a firm faith in the Law of Karma. "Those that hold on to the feet of the supreme Lord will cross the ocean of Births". "From the control of the senses arises the power to save oneself in seven births. "Death is but sleep". "Birth is only wakening from sleep." "Liberation can be secured through true wisdom." "Detachment is the means to come out of cycle of Births" "He who lives with righteousness will attain Heaven." "He who affords hospitality to a guest will go to the celestial region." "The debt owed to a person who aids us on his own, without being asked, cannot be discharged in full, even if both the worlds are offered to him in exchange."

Most translated Tamil Literature

The supremacy of the work can easily be gauged from the fact that it has been translated into many other Indian languages such as Hindi, Telugu, Malayalam, Bengali and Kannada and even into foreign languages such as English and French, German and Latin and has acquitted worldwide reputation. One noteworthy feature of Thirukkural is that composition and arrangement of chapters and the number of verses. In each have been preserved almost intact up to this time, as written by Valluvar initially. The first printed version of Thirukkural was published by an Englishman, Ellis in 1831, with the help of Tamil scholars.

Grand Memorials

A temple car like a memorial to Thiruvalluvar, called as "Valluvar Kottam" was built in Chennai - Nungambakkam in the year 1976. This monument complex consists of structures usually found in the south Indian temple including a temple car carved from three blocks of granite and a rectangular pond. The auditorium adjoining the memorial is one of the largest in Asia and can seat up to 4000 people. There is also a huge 133 foot tall statue of Thiruvalluvar erected at Kanyakumari at the southern most tip, next to the grand Swamy Vivekananda Rock memorial where the Ganga Sagar, Sindhu Sagar and the Indian Ocean converge. The 133 feet tall stature reflects the Thirukkural's 133 Chapters or adhikarams. There is also a stature of Thiruvalluvar outside the school of oriental studies in Russel Square, London. When I went to Myanmar in the year 1997, I saw a beautiful Thiruvalluvar temple on the banks of the river Iravadham.

Thirukkural - Leads us towards the path of righteousness:

Thirukkural is an essential part of our heritage, not only of the Tamils but the country as a whole. The book in a way bears evidence to the height of civilization and culture as well as intellectual attainments that HINDUS had reached nearly 2000 years ago.

Most translated Tamil Literature

The supremacy of the work can easily be gauged from the fact that it has been translated into many other Indian languages such as Hindi, Telugu, Malayalam, Bengali and Kannada and even into foreign languages such as English and French, German and Latin and has acquitted worldwide reputation. One noteworthy feature of Thirukkural is that composition and arrangement of chapters and the number of verses. In each have been preserved almost intact up to this time, as written by Valluvar initially. The first printed version of Thirukkural was published by an Englishman, Ellis in 1831, with the of Tamil Scholars.

❑

Rath Yatras—Bring Unity and Overwhelming Happiness

The Rath Yatras or temple car festivals are the oldest continuously celebrated religious events in India. Temple cars are basically chariots that are used to carry idols of gods and goddesses. The rathas are driven manually viz. pulled with the help of ropes by thousands of devotees. These beautifully decorated chariots, called Thiru Their in Tamil, and are a visual delight on wheels. Every year, during a particular period these splendidly decorated chariots of gods role down the streets accompanied by the devotees who chant Ved-mantras or recite shlokas or sing bhajans and namsankeertanams.

During these festivals, children are seen on the streets dragging miniature versions of the chariots with tiny idols installed on them. Shops and houses are decorated with flowers, lights and rangolis. Special dishes and sweets are prepared. Most of the people refrain from eating non-vegetariain food. One of the basic and significant features of rathotsav is that it brings people together under one common bond of unity. Various castes, communities, customs and traditions are found joyfully assimilated in all these rath yatras.

Tamil literature, specially the dewarams and prabhandams, mention about these ancient car festivals in several temple towns such as Thiruvarur, Srivilliputhur, Thiruvannamalai and Chidambaram. In Tamil Nadu as many as 515 wooden temple cars are taken out for procession every year. The chariot of Thiruvarur is said to be the biggest one in size. It is 96 feet tall and weighs more than three hundred tonnes. The thought content and the concept behind the ritual are also wonderful. According to Vedic faith, the human body is the chariot and the soul is the deity installed in the chariot. Wisdom guided by the soul acts as the chariot puller so as to pull the wheels of life in the right direction.

Thiruvannamalai Arunachaleshwar Mandir possesses a huge wooden chariot for procession. Inside this temple, Raman Maharishi performed his spiritual sadhana throughout his life. The Chidambaram Nataraja temple celebrates the chariot festival twice a year—one during July month for Aani Thirumanjanam and another during the winter, known as the Margazhi Thiruvadhirai utsav.

The impact of these Thiru Theirs rituals is really unique cutting across all societal barriers. Shri Karunanidhi, the former Chief Minister of Tamil Nadu calls himself an atheist. Some years back, he constructed a memorial for Thiruvalluvar who composed 1330 verses of Thirukural. During the course of planning, Shri Karunanidhi instructed the architects to design the main structure in such a way that it resembled the rath or Thiru Their of Thiruvarur temple, which happens to be his birthplace. So the impact of rathotsavas penetrates even an atheist's mind. The impact is virtually unstoppable and tremendous, because these festivals are no simple rituals or routine affairs. They signify a phenomenon saturated with intense faith of all sections of the people. Of late, many more temples like the Kanchi and Palani have acquired golden rathas. Lord Sri Krishna of Udupi has a variety of rathas some embellished with silver and gold plates.

Every year in Puri Jagannath Temple, three huge chariots

are newly built for Sri Krishna, His elder brother Balaram and His younger sister Subhadra. Over 1000 logs of wood are brought from Daspalla and Ranpur forests and more than 100 carpenters work for two months constructing the three chariots. A local textile mill provides nearly 2000 meters of cloth each year and the chariots are radiantly decorated in colour. Very strong coconut ropes, 8 inches in diameter, are used by the devotees to pull the chariot along the procession route. The nails, brackets and fixtures are all made locally and the smiths work for a month on them. Idols are placed on the chariots that are upto 48 feet high and have 16 wheels. The mammoth wooden chariots carrying the three deities pulled by thousands of devotees from the temple in Puri to temple garden in nearby Gundichaghar, present a spectacular scene.

The Temple Cars move rhythmically with their towering silken canopies rising into the sky as numerous drums resound in joyous celebrations. People, young and old join the yatra with excitement on a full moon day, their eyes brightened, singing and dancing in the street, as if swimming in the ocean of joy, nectar and happiness.

As far back as human records and memory extends, the chariots of Lord Jagannath have rolled every year on the 10th day of the bright fortnight of Ashada (July) in the town of Puri. On the day of the journey, people get up early morning and offer prayers to Lord Jagannath. The entire yatra is symbolic of self humanisation by God who descending from the pedestal of glory joins the multitude of men, women and children at their level of mortal existence. Among the teeming pilgrims while they pull the chariot, there remains no difference of high and low whatsoever. All become equals before and in the company of Lord Jagannath. To top it all, the Lord Himself eats the food prepared by the lowest man. The entire festival is organised so as to strengthen the emotional bonds of the people and to re-establish the oneness of humanity.

The annual rath yatra of Lord Jagannatha in Gujarat has been going on for the last 133 years. Earlier, it used to be only in Ahmedabad but now it has spread all over the State. It is celebrated with devotion in a peaceful and joyous atmosphere.

Now-a-days, this event is celebrated all over the world, wherever Hindus are living, with gaiety and grandeur.

Taking inspiration from this ancient car festival, the Vishawa Hindu Parishad (VHP) organises rath yatras in socially backward areas. Local deities, Devi Parvati and Kartikeya are taken to villages in Tamil Nadu, Orissa, Rajasthan and Andhra in decorated chariots. This has created a feeling amongst the people living in those villages that since God himself has come to their doorstep, there remains no difference of higher and lower castes in the Hindu society. Due to these rath yatras, groups of people in Tamil Nadu who earlier had embraced alien faiths came back to Hinduism. In the same way, several thousands of converted Vanvasis came back to Hindu fold in Orissa and Rajasthan.

The people who participate in these spiritual, cultural and social extravaganzas feel the presence of God in them and enjoy their blissful lives. Lord Jagannath is the most loving and kind form of the Almighty. Even those who hardly understand the philosophy behind the rath yatra become free of many lifetime karmas just by seeing the cavalcade or by taking part in the festival. One may even attain liberation from the bondage of life and death due to the spiritual power of the presence of Lord Jagannath.

> The Temple Cars move rhythmically with their towering silken canopies rising into the sky as numerous drums resound in joyous celebrations. People, young and old join the yatra with excitement on a full moon day, their eyes brightened, singing and dancing in the street, as if swimming in the ocean of joy, nectar and happiness.

❑

Saint Ramalinga Adigalar—Eternal light is the symbol of Knowledge, Care, Concern and Compassion

A saint in the mould of great Indian tradition

During the nineteenth century, a phenomenon occurred in the world of spirituality. Marudur is a small village in Tamil Nadu located about 15 kms, south west of Neiveli, well known to the world as an area containing vast reserves of lignite. There lived a couple named Ramiah Pillai and Chinnammal, who were devoted to the God with deep faith in Shaiva *siddhanta*.

One day, when Ramiah Pillai was away from home, a saffron-clad saint came to his house. The guest was treated courteously and offered good dishes. Pleased immensely, at the time of departure the saint, blessed the lady of the house with some sacred ash (*vibhuti*) and uttered the following words. "You will beget a son, who will reveal the art of deathlessness, which will be a boon to the entire world". So saying, the saint disappeared. Though it is acknowledged as a remarkable event, its hidden meaning is to be understood from a higher plane. Days passed by and the lady gave birth to a male child on the fifth day of October 1823.

Early Life

Blessed by the divine grace, the beloved parents showered their love and affection on the darling child and brought him up with great care. The child was named 'Ramalingam'. Usually, in India children are named after some god. The common belief is that once they call out the name of their dear ones, they are induced to remember the God often.

In Hinduism, it is a tradition to take a new born child to the temple and offer prayers before the deity and invoke His Blessings for the child. So, when the child was five months old, the parents took him to Chidambaram temple to offer their grateful prayers. As usual the priest lit the camphor and offered it to the Lord at the sanctum sanctorum. As soon as the vision appeared, the child laughed loudly and gazed at it for a few seconds. What did that suggest? One has to understand that the effulgence of the inner light of grace (*Arut Jothi*) has been realised by the child as soon as the outer light came within his visibility.

This pleasant experience has been expressed in some of the poems edited by the saint subsequently. Some of the excerpts are given below: "No sooner the Light was perceived, happiness prevailed on me. The sweet nectar was tasted by me as soon as the Great Light (*Arutperunjothi*) became visible". It is quite natural that the inner light is omniscient, and anyone having a mastery over it can enjoy happiness with a blissful state.

Years rolled down. The elder brother grew and he showed some interest in looking after the family, and as Chennai was considered to be the place, where he could have a better career. The family shifted to Chennai.

Divine Grace

When Ramalingam was five years old, Sabhapati, his elder brother, decided to formally educate his sibling but the kid showed a deep disinclination towards formal education. On the other hand, he preferred visits to the local Kandasamy temple. Ramalingam relented on the condition that he is given a separate room of his own. Now, in the solitary confines of this room, he set up a mirror and in front of it he lighted a lamp. With these as aids he relentlessly meditated and this was the beginning of the young boy's spiritual journey. The first reward came in the form of a vision of Lord Muruga.

His elder brother Sabhapati was a learned scholar and *upanyasaka* (one who tells religious stories). It so happened that once Ramalingam had to substitute for his brother at an *upanyasam* session. His brilliant exposition and uninterrupted flow of words while enunciating a verse from the *Periyapuranam* by Shaivism, an epic poem by Sekkizhar narrating the episodes connected with the 63 Nayanars amazed the audience. Later, his brother also acknowledged the mental and spiritual superiority of his younger brother. Totally averse to money, he was later on to shun food and even sleep. He started renouncing the world from the age of thirteen.

Ramalinga Swamy, as he was known by now, gained further spiritual experiences from his inner soul. He was able to awaken himself within by lighting a lamp. The grace of God was showered on him. Sitting before a lamp, he concentrated his thoughts on a certain spot in the mirror, where the brilliance of the lamp fell and he used to be lost in deep meditation. By the divine grace so obtained Ramalinga Swamy was blessed with the knowledge of all arts and skills and gifted with the ability and talent to perform wonderful deeds. Then he shifted himself to a village called Karungali in south Arcot District near Neiveli.

Hot Sun and Shadow of a Tree

During this period he wrote his spiritual experience in the form of 6000 poems. This divine composition of poems is called Thiru *Arutpa*. The Annamalai University has published a commentary for all the 6000 poems of Saint Ramalinga Swamy. The Madras University has published a book on *Arutperun Jothi*.

One of the poems of *Thiru Arutpa* explains as to how the happiness prevailing in the outer world is only a fraction of the inner happiness as an outcome of divine experience.

"During the hot summer at noon, a traveller after waiting

for a long distance comes in sight of a green tree full of branches and green leaves.

He sits under the shadow of the tree and thereby he is relieved of his tiredness and fatigue. What will be his feeling and appreciation about the green shade of the tree?

How glad will he be if begets a sweet, ripe fruit there to eat?

Nearby he sees a stream flowing with sweet cold water surrounded on either bank with colourful flowers emanating sweet fragrance bringing solace not only to the eyes but also to his mind.

He now feels that he is seated on a green meadow from where he takes rest.

The sweet breeze around him brings more comfort and thus he feels very fresh now with new gains and forgets all previous miseries.

The divine experience the saint acquired with the union of the Lord surpasses all such happiness prevailing in the outer world".

Centre for True Knowledge and Compassion

Based upon his divine experience, Swamy ji gave some *mantras*. He wanted his disciples to show*Jeevakarunyam* – compassion to all living beings. He established, Sathya Dharma Salai, in Vadalur. *Annadhan* was given to all the visitors without any distinction. He propagated the idea of vegetarianism. He was against the killing of animals for the sake of food. He encouraged the service of feeding the poor as the highest form of worship.

Ramalinga Swamy constructed a temple called the Sathya Gnana Sabhai. It is a hall of true knowledge. He said God of this temple is "Arul Perum Jothi" (eternal light). It is the symbol of knowledge, mercy and compassion.

The oil lamp lit by him is kept perpetually burning. He said that our inner soul is blinded by seven veils. Greediness, selfishness, ego, jealousy, enmity, lust and vengeance are the seven evils preventing us in the path of eternal bliss.

There are seven cotton fabric screens, representing the

seven factors that prevent a soul from realising its true nature. During the time of Aarathi, Deepa Aradhana, all the seven cotton screens in different colours are opened one by one and finally the devotee gets the *darshan* of the *Supreme Light*.

Ramalinga Swamy delivered the message through lectures, essays, heart melting poems and melodious songs. He insisted on the universal spiritual aspects of religion. He made an indelible mark in the religious history of India when he came out openly against the caste differences and the negative impact it had on society.

Ramalinga Swamy raised the flags of brotherhood on his one room residence at Siddhi Valakam in Mettukuppam. In an attempt to redress the situation, he established the Samarasa Suddha Sanmarga Satya Sangam.

He gave his last and most famous lecture, addressing the audience to look into the "nature of powers that lie beyond us and move us" and asking them to meditate on the lighted lamp. Saint Ramalinga Swamy is respected as "Siddhar" who attained *moksha* on January 30, 1874.

Thus, the saint Ramalinga Swamigal propagated the worship of the inner light in each human being and living being as *Arutperum Jothi*. There are about one thousand Sanmarga Sangams in Tamil Nadu and other bordering states like Kerala, Karnataka and Andhara Pradesh where people worship the light.

Atmosphere for Inculcating Values

In the year 1972, Mananeeya Madavarao Muley, the then all India *adhikari* of RSS visited this Ashram. As the district Pracharak of RSS, I took him to the Satya Gnana Sabai (hall of true knowledge), Dharma Sabai and Siddhivalagam.

He was impressed by the symbolic removal of seven screens or hurdles and finally worshipping the *'eternal light'*. He met the secretary of the *mutt* and had a long discussion. He specially told them that the Ashram is having a good atmosphere to give *sanskars* like brotherhood. Later on, after some years, RSS conducted its annual training camp called

OTC at the place. Mananeeya Rajju Bhaiya also visited the place and appreciated the role of the Ashram in spreading the message of Swamy ji.

<u>Centre for Ture Knowledge and Compassion</u>

He gave his last and most famous lecture, addressing the audience to look into the "nature of powers that lie beyond us and move us" and asking them to meditate on the lighted lamp. Thus, the saint Ramalinga Swamigal propagated the worship of the inner light in each human being and living being as *Arutperum Jothi*.

❑

Kashi Vishwanath Darshan—Most Sacred Place of Worship

Early morning on Mahashivaratri Day, I stood in a long queue to have the darshan of Kashi Vishwanath in Varanasi. There were several converging queues of devotees who thronged through different lanes surrounding the temple. The temple is reached through a narrow street flanked by a colourful market. The temple stands on the western bank of the holy river Ganga and is one of the twelve Jyotirlingas. Hindus from all over the world have an ardent desire to visit this shrine at least once in their life time. I was told by elderly people back home that most of the leading Hindu saints over the times, including Adi Shankaracharya, Ramakrishna Paramhansa, Swami Vivekananda, Goswami Tulsidas, Swami Dayananda Saraswati and Guru Nanakdev had visited the temple. They considered Kashi Viswanath temple as one of the most sacred places dedicated to Lord Shiva. Being founded on the Trident of the Lord, it is the holiest place of Hindus.

Most of the people standing in the queue for darshan already had take bath in the river Ganga. Some of them were standing wearing wet clothes as they believed that the darshan of Kashi Vishwanath soon after taking bath in the Ganga is an act of great religious merit. There is also a tradition that after visiting Kashi the pilgrimage would include a visit to the temple at Rameshwaram in south India, where people take the Ganga water to perform prayers at the temple. Due to the immense popularity and holiness of this shrine, a large number of temples across the nation have been built with similar names. In Tamil Nadu there is Thenkashi (Southern Kashi), in Chennai there is Kashi mode, Uttar Kashi in northern India is also well known to all.

A foreigner was standing next to me in the queue. I asked him as to what made him visit this temple town. He was a German and was studying Sanskrit language and the Vedas. "The Shanti Mantra-Om Shanti, Shanti Shanti-inspired me" he replied. I asked him, do you know the meanings of the mantra. He told me, "Om Shanti" means calm and peaceful mind. We should not get trouble from ourselves, from others and finally from external forces. By reciting the mantra, three times we become quiet, clam& peaceful with ourselves, with others and with nature. Our mind starts feeling oneness with the God. The vast span of Ganga River gives me a broader outlook. So I visit this temple town often. I know this is the oldest city of the world, with 3500 years of documented history."

A guide was accompanying the foreigner. A student from Tamil Nadu who also was standing in the queue requested the guide to tell the story of the temple. The guide became enthusiastic by seeing good number of people paying attention to him. He narrated the history of the place in his own way thus: "Varanasi becomes immensely sacred due to the presence of Mahadev Shiva from times immemorial. Shiva gives a never ending joyous spirit to the people. This ancient Shiva temple has been mentioned in Puranas including Kashi Khanda of Skanda Purana. Varanasi has been a sacred place since ages. It is mentioned in the Vedas, Puranas, and the epics of Ramayana and Mahabharata and many Jain and Buddhist texts. Kashi has been a great centre of education. Students were taught the

Vedas, the Upanishads and other schools of philosophy and religious thought in the ashrams or study centres that existed on the bank of river Ganga.

From the Himalayas down to the plains of the Gangetic Valley and beyond from the Narmada down South upto Kanyakumari all along the banks of river Ganga, Narmada, Mahanadi, Cauvery, Vagai, Thamiravaruni, Shiva is worshipped in many forms. So profound is the connection of Shiva with the mountains and the river Ganga that He is associated with such descriptions as the Dweller of the Mountains and the Upholder of Ganga viz. Gangadhara.

The Chinese traveler Huen Tsang, who visited Varanasi in the 7th century, saw hundreds of Hindu temples, thousands of priests and ascetics, with ashes smeared over their bodies, practicing penances to come out of the circle of births and deaths. Among other things, Huen Tsang also described the existence of a statue of Shiva that was 30 meters high."

Spell bound with the narration of the guide, the devotees were inching towards the temple. Some people purchased tea for him to refresh. The guide continued the description of historical events with more earnestness. Said he,"Varanasi suffered a lot during the Muslim invasion from 12th century onward. Kashi, being a religious city of great antiquity with idol worship as the regular tradition, Muslim rulers destroyed the whole thing as the torch-bearers of Islam. Reconstruction of the temple started soon after. This was demolished by Qutubuddin Aibak. After his death, the temple was again rebuilt. In 1351, it was again destroyed by another Muslim ruler and was rebuilt again by Hindus. Aurangzeb ordered its demolition in 1669 and constructed the Gyanvapi mosque in its place, which still exists alongside the temple. Traces of the old temple can be seen behind the mosque. The existent temple was built by the Maratha ruler Ahilya Bai Holkar of Indore in 1780. The temple tower was gold plated with the 1000 kg of gold donated by Maharaja Ranjeet Singh of Punjab in 1836.Thus Muslim rulers destroyed the Kashi Vishwanath temple several times. But they could not destroy the spirit and the religious fervour of the Hindu society. Varanasi continued to thrive as a city of Hindu learning and centre of Hindu pilgrimage even during its testing times. In the midst of all turmoil, many saints and sages re-awakened the spirit and faith of the people. The religious emotions of Hindus always flowed like the perennial river Ganga. Nobody could stop the devotion and dedication of Hindus."

By this time we had reached the temple. There was a huge crowd of devotees surging from all sides. Even to have a glimpse of the Shivalinga, everyone was struggling. Maha Aarti was perfomed. People were praying with great devotion and heartwarming passion. I was just standing near the sanctum sanctorum. More and more ardent devotees were pouring into the shrine. Temple registers a stunning record of 10000 visitors every day. The local administration and the police guards were expecting at least 10 lakh people on the day of Mahashivaratri. The deity is most powerful. He is the god of all gods. A huge number of devotees visit the place with enormous faith in Vishwanathji. The main shrine is very small. People were expressing a desire for building a more spacious shrine with adequate facility for worship.

After darshan, I boarded the Shiva Ganga Express train and returned to Delhi. I was touched by the matchless devotion of people. My mind was filled with spiritual thoughts. The city of Varanasi continues to fascinate the world with its religiosity and rich cultural heritage even today. No city in India arouses religious emotions of Hindus as much as Kashi does.

> The Chinese traveler Huen Tsang, who visited Varanasi in the 7th century, saw hundreds of Hindu temples, thousands of priests and ascetics, with ashes smeared over their bodies, practicing penances to come out of the circle of births and deaths. Among other things, Huen Tsang also described the existence of a statue of Shiva that was 30 meters high."

❑

Madurai Meenakshi Amman Temple—The Greatest Gift of our Forefathers

A tradition of divine birthday festivities

* Deep pooja by 10,000 mothers
* Worship of cows
* Cleaning of the temple by 1000 volunteers
* Annadanam

THE Hindu Temple Protection Committee recently celebrated the birthday of goddess Meenakshi in Madurai. Over 10,000 women performed the 'Deep Puja' (Worship of the Lamp) cutting across all caste barriers, with all devotion. The spirit of unity was evident during their collective efforts to celebrate the birthday of the Divine Mother. Volunteers numbering 1000 belonging to a devotees' forum called 'Bhaktar Pevavai' cleaned the temple with water and decorated it with kolams. It is a massive task requiring dedication by each and every karyakarta. The worshippers' forum trains the workers with a spiritual bent of mind. True strength lies in submission which permits one to dedicate his life, through devotion to something beyond himself.

Beautiful Towers

Meenakashi Amman Temple is one amongst the most important temples of the country. The temple structure sprawls in an area of 45 acres. The complex comprises 12 superlative gopurams. These tall towers rise to a height of more than 50 meters. Apart from this, there are two golden towers dedicated to the presiding deities. These beautiful temple towers are elaborately sculptured, painted and decorated. There are 30 million colourful carvings and gypsum images around the temple. The tallest tower rises to the extent of 170 feet. The main sanctum sanctorum is believed to be more than 2500 years old.

Madurai never sleeps

Tamil literature describes Madurai as the city of nectar. It is located on the banks of the Vaigai River. Once it was the capital of Pandyan rulers and has been a centre of learning and pilgrimage ever since. It is the most vibrant city of Tamil Nadu during day time as well as during night. Thirugnana Sambhandar, the famous saint of Shaiva siddhanta, mentioned this temple as early as the 7th century and described the lord as Aalavai Iraivan. The colossal structure of the temple was constructed by Kulasekara Pandyan. It has a huge dimension of 254 by 237 meters. Having a history for thousands of years, the present structure of the Temple was erected during early 17th century.

From the debris it rises again

The temple was ransacked by the Muslim invader Malik Kafur in the year 1310 AD. and all the ancient structures were destroyed. The initiative to rebuild the temple was taken by the first Nayak king of Madurai. The most valuable contribution was made by King Thirumalai Nayak. He constructed several mandapas and stupas inside and outside the temple including the Vasanta Mandapam and the Aayiram Kaal Mandapam. The latter is a thousand pillared hall and is prominent due to its class sculptures. The hall is truly marvelous and definitely is worth visiting for its beautiful architecture.

Meenakshi Devi

Malayadwaja Pandya once was the King of Madurai. He was childless for long and performed an elaborate yajna, (sacrificial rite before the sacred fire, the Agni) to beget a child. To the wonder of all, a girl child emerged from the fire. The Queen Kanchanamala was thrilled to see the baby and took the child and embraced her and put her on her lap. This happened during the Tamil month of Thai (January) on the day of Magh Nakshatra. The King, the queen and the people were very happy. The birthday celebrations for new arrival, later revealed as goddess Minakshi, were marked by extensive poojas and recitations of Nama Sankeertanas. 108 cows were worshipped with naivedyam, pooja and mangal aarti. All visitors were offered good food.

Meenakshi Thiru Kalyanam

As per the belief of the devotees, Madurai is the city where lord Sundareswar had married the goddess Meenakshi. The name Sundareswara means the Beautiful Shiva and Meenakshi means, the Fish Eyed Goddess. Madurai temple is regarded as one of the most sacred places of Devi Parvati, others being Kamakshi of Kanchipuram and Kashi Visalakshi of Varanasi.

The marriage ceremony is replicated each year with pomp and pageantry and in all its magnificence and splendour to the great delight of devotees. Mahavishnu had visited Madurai as brother of Devi Meenakshi and formally gave the bride to Shiva. Lord Brahma performed the marriage rituals with Vedic mantras. The marriage scene is carved beautifully as a shilpa sculpture on one of the pillars. The belief is thatLord Mahavishnu comes across the Vaigai River from the nearby temple of Azhagarkovil each year to participate in the festivities. The festival that attracts the devotees most is the Meenakshi Kalyanam, popularly known as Chithirai festival.

The sthalapakshi (local bird) is the parrot. People can see the parrot sitting on the shoulders of Meenakshi. Temple authorities maintain many parrots in and around the temple. This kshetra is called as *kadamba van,* the forest of the Kadamb trees.

Potramaraikulam (Golden Lotus Tank)

Within the temple complex is located the Potramaraikulam, a consecrated pond, where the devotees take bath in the holy water, before entering the main shrine. The name Potramaroikulam suggests the pond with a golden lotus. The area around this tank was the meeting place of the Tamil Sangam, the ancient academy of poets. This academy judged the worth of any work of literature presented before it. The pond served as an evaluator for reviewing the worth of a new literature.

Velli Ambalam

A silver statue of Nataraja is placed near the sanctum sanctorum. It is called Velli Ambalam or the silver abode of Shiva. Usually, Lord Nataraja performs the dance by raising his left leg. A story goes that a visiting devotee was moved emotionally seeing the Lord in that posture. In his wisdom, he felt that lifting of the left leg was tiresome for the Lord. So he prayed to the lord, to change it with the right leg. Seeing his true devotion, Lord Nataraja, changed the posture, and fulfilled the prayer of the devotee. Nataraja here is seen with a difference.

Greatest Gift

The Meenakshi Temple in Madurai has a long and great history. It is known for its superb sculpture. The temple is an architectural marvel displaying the most exquisite artistry in design and execution. The Meenakshi Amman Temple has been nominated for the new Seven Wonders of the World. Thousands of devotees come every day to pay their obeisance to Goddess Meenakshi and return fulfilled.

> Once, the celebrated Indologist Max Muller had said that "If I were asked under what sky the human mind has most fully developed some of its choicest gifts, I should point to India." There is no doubt that Madurai Meenakshi Temple is one of the greatest gifts of our forefathers to the present and future generations.

❑

Bhrahadheeshwara Temple— An Architectural Wonder

A thousand years ago, Raja Raja-I of the Chola dynasty, built a majestic temple for Lord Shiva at Thanjavur (Tanjore), Tamil Nadu. Called the Peruvuidayar Kovil, or the Brihadeeswarar Temple, or sometimes the Rajarajeswaram it is on rolls of the UNESCO heritage sites as part of the circuit called "Great Living Chola Temples". The Tamil Nadu government recently organised a grand function, spanning over five days, to celebrate the millennium of its consecration. A scintillating Bharatnatyam recital by 1,000 artistes, led by the eminent danseuse Padma Subrahmanyam, took the cream of the cake. A host of events including exhibitions, cultural shows, seminars and deliberations were also organised to mark the occasion.

Tamil Nadu remains a wonderful repository of classical India; be it the temple architecture or dance or music, both vocal and instrumental. It hosts the oldest living temples in India, which remained unaffected by the iconoclasm of the Turks, the Mughals and the Bahmani invaders. In ancient India, these temples were not merely centres of religion, but were also the abode of art, Architecture, culture, literature and vocational training. The Brihadeeswarar Temple stands as a reminder of our great culture: art, architecture, religion and language. It also symbolizes the great wealth and powets of the Cholas, who extended their empire across the Indian Ocean.

The construction of this 'Big Temple' began in 1003 CE and was completed in six years before being consecrated in 1010 CE. The unique archaeological feature of the temple is its Vimana (temple tower) standing 216 feet tall. The summit stone weighing about eighty tons was dragged on to the top through a slope path from a distant Village, called 'Sarapallam'. It rises over the sanctum, on a square base about a hundred feet dominating the whole structure. Its shadow never falls on the ground.

The valiant king Raja Raja-I, who reigned between 985 and 1014 CE, was renowned for conquests on land and sea. He always found peace at the feet of Lord Shiva. Construction of the Brihadeeshwara temple coincided with a visible shift in his policies from military expansion to the consolidation of internal administration. But, neither he nor his illustrious son Rajendra I (who built the famous Shiva temple at Gangaikonda Cholapuram, similar in design to Brihadeeshwara temple) neglected either the external or the internal security of their empire, unlike some others who weakened the martial spirit of India by neglecting the art and practices of war making.

A distinct feature of the Brihadeeshwara temple is the magnificent monolith Nandi bull, the mount of Lord Shiva, facing the temple tower. The shrines of goddess Brihanayaki, Ganapati, Subhramanya, Dakshinamurty and Nataraja are finely carved. The corridor surrounding the sanctum is a treasure house of Chola paintings and sculpture. The walls of this cave-like corridor were plastered with lime and used as large canvases for painting. The paintings, which have survived the vagaries of time and a seventeenth century coat of paint, are very beautiful in detail, colour and finesse.

The story of Sundaramurthy Nayanar reaching Kailash on a white elephant is depicted on a wall. On the other Karuvur Thevar, the Guru of Raja Raja is portrayed in an impressive manner. While the sculptures of Shiva in this corridor are imposing and colossal, the series of eighty one dance poses are no less superb illustrations of the Natya Sashtra.

There is an interesting and popular story about the deep personal interest that the King evinced in the construction of the temple. It is said that one day, when the chief sculptor was deeply absorbed in chiseling the huge Nandi, King Raja Raja Chola went and stood by his side. The sculptor, thinking that it was his boy attendant standing by his side ordered him to prepare a pan (betel leaf with araca nut and lime). The king calmly obliged, folded a couple of betel leaves and handed it over to the sculptor who received it without seeing the hands that supplied them. Chewing the pan in his mouth, the sculptor started uttering words of praise, appreciating the king who planned this unique monument. Later, he asked 'his attendant' to bring the spittoon near him. The king silently obeyed. When the sculptor raised his head after spitting the chewed betel leaves, he was terribly shocked to see the great Raja Raja Chola standing in front of him. Immediately, he touched the feet of the king with tears and offered apologies to the emperor, in a voice choked with emotion. The king, with a smiling face, lifted him up and consoled him by telling that it was a rare privilege for him to serve the sculptor whose hands chiselled the sculptures of the magnificent temple. Raja Raja Chola, though a worshiper of Shiva was tolerant to other religions.

He endowed and built temple of Maha Vishnu. He granted a village to the Buddhist Vihara at Nagappattinam. The Brihadeeswara temple was not an act of royal fancy. It is iconic of the glory of Tamil Saiva Siddhanta. Amongst two principal schools of Bhakti cult prevalent in South India, Saivism has a larger following.

In Tamil districts of Sri Lanka Saivism holds an

unchallenged sway. In Saiva Siddhanta Shiva is believed to exercise the functions of creation, protection, and destruction. These functions He is said to discharge with a view to releasing the struggling souls from the bondage of karma, and present unto them the ultimate knowledge of Shiva. The goal of individual souls is to realise that it is made of Shiva-Tatva (element of Shiva), and though not merging in Shiva, remain at its feet like a beloved child. The icon of Lord Nataraja is symbolic of Saiva Siddhanta. Temple worship is an indispensable part of this Siddhanta. That might explain why Tamilians carry an image of being orthodox and are scrupulous temple goers.

Raja Raja Chola's reign represents the sublime height achieved by Saivism in southern India. This was made possible by the surge of Shiva devotion brought in by the Nayanar saints during the previous centuries. The heart melting hymns (Devaram) to Lord Shiva by Sambandar, Appar and Sundaramurthy as well as Manikkavasagar who wrote Tiruvasagam in the 9th century are worth listening to. They, in reality were the pioneers of the Bhakti movement that later swept across other parts of India in the medieval period. Raja Raja Chola was an extra ordinarily powerful king and a grand monarch of southern India. His army crossed the ocean by ships and conquered many islands. His was a versatile personality.

It is a matter of pride that Tanjore temple attracted the appreciation of UNESCO for its art and architecture. The Brihadeeswara Temple is a shining jewel in the crown of Bharatmata. No doubt, it is Tamil Nadu's precious contribution to the pride of India. Let us all celebrate this thousand year old architectural wonder.

❑❑❑